MW00807975

MYTHS AND MYSTERIES SERIES

MYTHS AND MYSTERIES

OF
NEW HAMPSHIRE

TRUE STORIES
OF THE UNSOLVED AND UNEXPLAINED

MATTHEW P. MAYO

gpp

Guilford, Connecticut

For Jennifer . . . for always and for everything

To buy books in quantity for corporate use
or incentives, call **(800) 962-0973**
or e-mail **premiums@GlobePequot.com.**

Map by Alena Joy Pearce © Morris Book Publishing, LLC
Project editor: Lauren Szalkiewicz
Layout: Sue Murray
Cover photo: Jennifer Smith-Mayo

Library of Congress Cataloging-in-Publication Data is available on file.

ISBN 978-0-7627-7227-8

10 9 8 7 6 5 4 3 2 1

CONTENTS

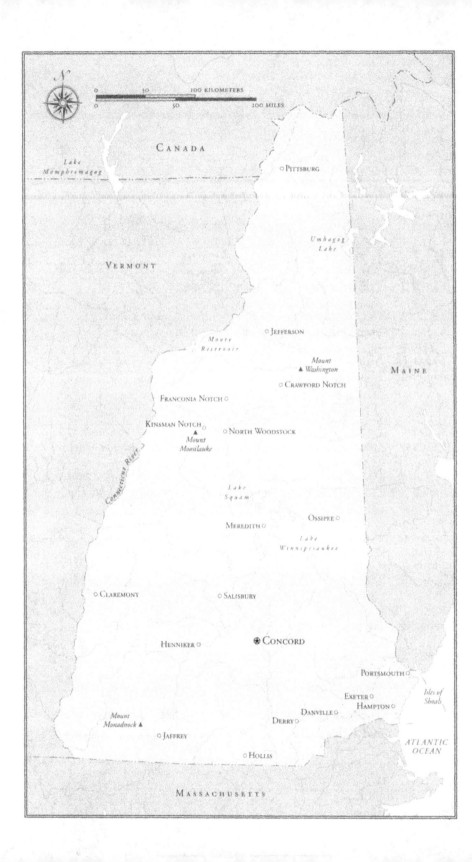

ACKNOWLEDGMENTS

My sincere thanks to Erin Turner for being such a great editor and chum. And much thanks and appreciation to Richard Boutwell and the Jaffrey Historical Society; Loren Coleman and the International Cryptozoology Museum; Douglas Copeley and the New Hampshire Historical Society; Roland Goodbody and the Milne Special Collections and Archives Department of the University of New Hampshire Library; and Cheryl Lassiter and the Hampton Historical Society and Tuck Museum.

Most of all, I thank my wife, Jennifer Smith-Mayo, for her fine images, and for conducting all the historical image research and procurement for my books (and so much more!). And for her continuing ceaseless patience, unfailing good humor, and the warmest of smiles. You're a wonder!

INTRODUCTION

The White Mountain State, the Switzerland of America, the Mother of Rivers, the Granite State, all most apt monikers. And yet, no nickname can begin to adequately describe the natural and man-made wonders that make New Hampshire such a singular place, and her people as equally distinct.

Not only does New Hampshire have the Northeast market cornered on all the raw, rugged beauty nature has to offer, but she bubbles with a rich and often mysterious human history that long predates white European settlement. This springs from a time when Native Americans looked to the slopes of what is now known as Mount Washington, and whispered "Agiocochook"—"Home of the Great Spirit."

Or later, when a North Woods logger glanced up from his task to see a massive, shaggy man-beast spying on him from the edge of the clearing. Or when notorious pirates buried their plunder along the Isles of Shoals. Or today, when tourists visit the New Hampshire Historical Society and puzzle over the inexplicable egg known as the Mystery Stone. . . .

Denizens of the Granite State embrace their episodes of odd history, mysterious happenings, and downright suspect claims, warts and all, and often elevate them to lofty heights. Such as erecting a marker on Route 3 in Franconia Notch in honor of Betty and Barney Hill, who were run aground by a UFO in 1961—and became the first officially documented alien abductees in the United States. Or by celebrating and marketing the fact that Eunice "Goody" Cole is the only woman to be convicted of witchcraft in the state. Or by maintaining a firm hold on the symbolic memory of the Old Man of the Mountain, despite the fact he's now so much collapsed cliff-face.

Fiercely proud of who they are and where they live, Granite Staters temper this inherent optimistic vein of Yankee hucksterism with a rugged spirit as unyielding as the very granite on which they tread. Anyone who doubts that need only recall those oft-quoted words of favored son General John Stark, as rugged and admirable a Granite Stater as they come: "Live free or die; Death is not the worst of evils."

With the core of such a sentiment worn in plain sight for all to see (on every license plate!), is there a more fertile setting than New Hampshire in which the good, bad, and ugly of strange and mysterious stuff might germinate and blossom? Not hardly. In New Hampshire, it seems you can't wander more than a few feet in any direction, turn over any rock, inquire of any stranger, or thumb through any old book without finding a headscratcher that's just as apt to be a howling hoax as a qualified mystery.

Sometimes the facts are muddy; sometimes they're just buried under layers of opinion. But sometimes vague notions bloom into the best stories of all. Are they true? Perhaps. Who's to say? Where appropriate I spiced up various tales with a pinch of narrative license, adding dialogue that we can guess would have taken place had we been there to witness the events. Also, where necessary, I have made efforts to alter names to protect reputations that might suffer the sneers of skeptics.

Most of all, I had a whole lot of fun researching and writing the book. It took me to places I'd not visited, and introduced me to historic characters I never would have met (and some I don't ever care to again!). Witches, pirates, ghosts, vicious storms, grave robbers, lost treasure, thieves, killers, aliens—who wouldn't find such a rogues' gallery fascinating? After all, here be monsters . . . and myths and mysteries!

—Matthew P. Mayo
Autumn, 2013

CHAPTER 1

Abducted!

The Betty & Barney Hill UFO Incident . . . and Other Granite State Alien Tales

The evening of September 19, 1961, found Betty and Barney Hill, residents of Portsmouth, New Hampshire, heading south from a vacation in Canada, where they'd visited Niagara Falls and Montreal. News of a hurricane tracking into the Northeast had prompted them to cut short their trip by a few days. At ten thirty that night, while driving through New Hampshire's Franconia Notch along a particularly dark stretch of Route 3, Betty happened to glance out the car's rear window. She noticed a strange light in the sky, perhaps a star, but it looked as if it was following them. She watched it for a few seconds and then mentioned it to her husband, Barney, who was driving.

They both thought it odd, but guessed it was a reflection, or perhaps an optical illusion. Yet the strange light persisted—and then it drew closer, and looked to be a series of lights. By that time, Betty had retrieved their binoculars from the backseat, and when she finally focused on the odd lights, what she saw tightened her throat.

The thing looked an awful lot like an airplane. After all, it sported windows and flashing lights. But an airplane flying that low? And following them? Perhaps the pilot was in trouble. She described what she was seeing and Barney slowed the car, his brow furrowed in concern. He knew Betty wasn't prone to flights of fancy, so there might well be something to what she was saying. But what?

Meanwhile, Betty kept an eye on the odd sight and with each second that passed, she grew more convinced that what she was seeing wasn't any aircraft. At least not one she had ever seen. Barney agreed. He'd been in World War II, he'd witnessed his share of airplanes, and this thing didn't move like any he'd ever seen. As he checked the lights in the mirror, he saw that the thing was wide and fast, and moved erratically. And it seemed to be gaining on them. So what was it?

Intrigued and not sensing danger, he pulled over to the side of the road at Clark's Field, just past the Indian Head Resort near Mount Pemigewasset. They climbed out of the car and the object was close enough that they both could plainly see it was some sort of massive flying disc. Staring up at the amazing sight, Betty handed Barney the binoculars. When Barney focused in on the strange object, similar to Betty earlier, he too didn't want to trust his eyes.

Driving home through Franconia Notch on the night of September 19–20, 1961, Betty and Barney Hill underwent an experience that made them the first officially reported UFO abductees in the United States.

"What do you see?" Betty asked, squinting up at the lights. Barney kept staring through the binoculars at the strange thing, but Betty could tell something was wrong. He looked shaken. "Barney, what is it?"

He wanted to tell her he'd seen a number of people—or something like them. And they were watching him just as he was watching them!

Finally, in a shaky voice, Barney shouted, "I don't believe it!" as the huge disc zoomed even closer. It was nearly above them now, no more than eighty feet off the ground. Barney tugged at the binoculars so hard he broke the leather strap as he bolted back toward the car. "Get in the car! We have to get out of here!"

He fired up the ignition and they rooster-tailed roadside gravel as they resumed their previous direction, speeding south-ward on Route 3. Their increasing speed didn't seem to matter, for they soon realized they couldn't outrun the thing. Those lights were closer than ever, pulsing and hovering directly above them.

In the midst of their sudden grip of panic and fear, Betty shouted, "Do you hear that?" A strange, incessant buzzing sound emanated from the rear of their car. At the same time, a creep-ing drowsiness overcame them. For the next few minutes they struggled to remain awake.

Through it all, Barney continued to navigate the car toward North Woodstock, then finally onto a dirt road, almost as if they were somehow directed to the spot. That's when they knew no more . . . until a short time later, when that buzzing noise from the trunk awakened them. They struggled back to consciousness just in time to see the massive flying disc circle over them before departing into the night sky. But it hadn't been a short time later.

Despite feeling drowsy and cloudy-headed, Betty and Bar-ney roused themselves enough to continue their journey, slowly gaining more clarity with each mile that passed. By the time they arrived in Portsmouth, it was five o'clock in the morning. That's when they realized that their wristwatches had stopped. The Hills also discovered that somehow they had lost three hours on their homeward journey from Franconia Notch to Portsmouth—the four-hour trip had taken seven.

The next day they found a series of concentric circles dotting the surface of their car's trunk. When they roved a compass over the spots, the needle spun erratically. Yet more alarming was the state of Betty's dress. In fine condition the day before, now the hem was ripped, fabric had been torn near the top of the zipper, and the lining had been damaged. (Later still, she would discover an odd, pink residue clinging to the fabric. The powdery substance would later be analyzed by five scientific laboratories, yet it remains unidentified today.)

They also discovered that Barney's leather shoes were so scraped and scarred, he was forced to buy a new pair. His pant legs were begrimed with some form of unidentified flora, and as time wore on, he developed a worrisome circle of wartlike growths near his groin that later became inflamed when he would undergo deep hypnosis. They were surgically removed and determined unidentifiable and not to be any form of venereal affliction.

Confused and curious, Betty telephoned the 100th Bomb Wing Strategic Air Command at Pease Air Force Base, in nearby Newington, New Hampshire. She offered a general overview of the incident, though Barney chose to omit mention of the figures he'd seen in the window of the strange craft. The Hills were contacted by Major Paul W. Henderson, who questioned them at length. He seemed particularly interested in the craft's winglike protuberances that the Hills described as having telescoped from opposite sides of the craft.

Betty and Barney would later find out that Pease Air Force Base's radar tracking system had registered what was classified as "an unknown" on the same night as their incident. The air force sent out two planes to track the unidentified craft—the pilots' reports are still classified today.

For two years after the incident, the Hills existed under increasing emotional stress that manifested itself in a number of ways, including horrific nightmares and mental fatigue. They felt as if they were both on the verge of remembering something, but were somehow blocked from recalling it. Out of desperation and anxiety about their own mental health, the Hills sought professional help and ended up under the care of renowned neuropsychiatrist Dr. Benjamin Simon.

In the days, weeks, months, and years that followed, Betty and Barney Hill would learn more than they ever could have imagined about that night. Not only would their discoveries inextricably alter their lives, they would alter the course of UFO studies the world over.

From January to June 1964, the Hills underwent a six-month series of deep medical hypnosis sessions conducted by Dr. Simon, a pragmatic man used to treating battle-weary soldiers. The Hills divulged their story, corroborating each other's accounts in ways neither of them could have known. Eventually they learned that they had been abducted by space aliens.

* * *

Under deep hypnosis, Betty recounted the events—alternately frightening and fascinating—that had befallen her. On that fateful night, the Hills had driven southward on Route 3, tracked from above by the frightening aircraft. Soon their car rolled to a stop at Russell Pond. The Hills seemed to have fallen into a deep trance, yet they could somehow still see and hear, as if drugged. What they could not do was prevent the eleven strange humanoid creatures from lifting them from the car and walking them in their trancelike state to the odd spacecraft that had dogged them through the mountains.

The beings, she said, were roughly five feet four inches tall, had gray skin, and wore beige suits that seemed to Betty to be uniforms. They all dressed alike, save for one, who wore black and to whom the others seemed to defer. Their hairless heads were bigger than those of humans, and oddly shaped, as though eggs stood on their narrow end. They sported almond-shaped eyes, slightly larger than humans', they had small, pug-like noses, and where ears should be there were instead holes.

Betty and Barney were led into the ship, where she gained consciousness enough to talk. Betty struggled briefly with them when they nudged Barney away from her. She shouted, begging them not to separate them. At this point, the being dressed in black, whom she took as the leader, spoke to her in English, though she recalled that at the time this did not surprise her. He told her that she and Barney were to be harmlessly examined and that keeping them together would only slow down the process.

She protested, begged them not to do whatever it was they had in mind, but her efforts proved to no avail. Much to her surprise, the creatures—by now she had guessed they were some sort of aliens from space—were oddly placating. One of the beings walked into the chamber in which Betty was being held. Along with the leader, this new being, whom Betty referred to in her hypnosis sessions as "the examiner," as with the leader, spoke to her in English. His proficiency with the language was stilted and Betty found it difficult at times to comprehend him. He said he wished to perform a number of quick tests that would help them learn the difference between earthlings and his own people.

They made her lie on a table and once again Betty was told that she would not be harmed. Then, as if she were on a dental visit, they beamed a glaring light on her and proceeded to examine her. First, the examiner snipped a thick lock of Betty's hair, then he inspected Betty's eyes, making slight noises, as if of approval or confirmation of something he had assumed.

He looked up her nose, in her ears, gently forced her mouth open wide, and examined her throat. All the while they examined her, they asked her questions about what humans ate, how long they lived, about reproduction, and a number of other topics anyone curious about another species might well ask. Though she was nervous, Betty answered them to the best of her knowledge.

The examiner then shifted his attention to her hands, and bent, flexed, and pulled her fingers, then trimmed fingernails and saved the clippings. After that, he held up what looked like a letter opener and scraped some of her skin onto a thin, filmy substance.

Though still terrified, Betty had by this time calmed, assuming that if this were the extent of the examination, then this frightening situation might somehow turn out better than she had any right to hope.

Just then the examiner and the leader, who had been assisting in the examination, approached her with a long, gleaming needle, which he stabbed into her navel. "It hurts!" she shouted "Make it stop, please stop this!" They did, then the leader passed his bony fingers over her eyes and the pain abated.

A short time later, the examiner left with his gathered information and samples. He returned and inspected her teeth. While he did so, he asked her why her teeth didn't come out. In this way, she found out that they must have examined Barney. She then explained that her husband had false teeth. Betty, still feeling addled but somehow coherent, cautiously inspected the room and conversed with the leader. He watched her as she picked up what looked to be a book. It was covered in odd symbols, which she assumed was his race's writing. He told her she was free to take the book home with her. This made her feel better, because it gave her hope that she would not be kept a prisoner on the strange ship.

"Where are you from?" she asked. The leader fiddled with something that blinked and illuminated what appeared to be a three-dimensional floating globe covered with stars, as if the very heavens themselves were mapped and charted in the air before her.

"Here," he said, pointing, and described the location of his home planet, the journey they took to get there, and told her that the region they were from was called the "Zeta Reticuli." Little did Betty know that this bit of information would prove most useful to her later.

Soon she was led from the room and met up with Barney, who was by then more coherent than he had been. He had obviously also undergone an ordeal, but he looked worse than she felt she did. As they were escorted from the ship, retracing the same route they had traveled on their way into the gleaming craft, the examiner, the leader, and a few of the others began arguing in their own language. The leader approached Betty and took the book from her, telling her that it had been decided that she would not be allowed to remember the incident. She told them that she was strong-willed and would do whatever it took to remember the strange encounter.

Once they reached the Hills' car, the leader told them that they should stand by it and watch the ship depart. They did, still feeling as if they were in an odd dream. Then Betty and Barney Hill climbed into their car and once more resumed their journey toward Portsmouth and home—and toward a future of unwanted infamy.

Two years after their life-altering event, during his series of deep hypnosis sessions with Dr. Simon, Barney Hill recalled genuine horror at seeing these strange beings, and corroborated Betty's account of the events, that they were indeed taken aboard the craft, and then separated. He was led to a room and told to climb upon an examination table. He was frightened enough that he kept his eyes closed for much of the coming examination. When he did open them he recalled, with horror, eyes that seemed as if they were pressing into his, as if they were disconnected from bodies.

Barney, like Betty, endured a number of procedures. His spine was inspected, and he thought that one of the creatures was counting his vertebrae. As with Betty, they also took skin scrapings and inspected his ears and mouth. Throughout the examination, he heard the creatures converse in a mumbling sort of language, and when they did attempt to communicate with him, he felt they were doing so in a telepathic way, and not using spoken language.

As with Betty's recounting of the event, Barney recalled being escorted from the ship and returned to their car, where they were urged to stand by and watch the ship depart.

During their sessions, Dr. Simon used deep-trance hypnotic regression therapy to help unlock what it was the Hills believed had happened to them that night. At the end of each session, he induced amnesia to protect them from recalling the traumatic events his sessions were dredging up, and he wanted to prevent them from discussing their individual experiences with each other.

Though a staunch skeptic of the possibility of the existence of UFOs, Dr. Simon concluded that the Hills' experiences were "singular psychological aberrations." He also admitted that his varied hypotheses failed to explain a number of elements of the detailed events they each related under hypnosis.

Another curious result that arose from the sessions has come to be regarded as the most important and credible piece of information from their entire experience. In one of those 1964 sessions, Betty described the detailed map of stars she was shown by the leader aboard the ship, and then created a hand-drawn version of it. At the time, Betty Hill's detailed array of stars was looked upon as a curiosity, but not of significance. At least not until 1969, when that very star cluster was identified in the heavens by astronomer Marjorie Fish. There was no way in 1964 that Betty could have known about the as-yet-undiscovered star cluster. The pattern was officially named the Fish-Hill Pattern, a name it bears to this day.

The Hills' story became public on October 25, 1965, in the *Boston Traveler* newspaper. For five days, the publication ran the headlining story, "Incident at Indian Head," detailing Betty and Barney's encounter and abduction. Though the journalist never bothered to speak with them, Betty later said most of his facts were, surprisingly, correct. A year later, John G. Fuller's blockbuster account, *The Interrupted Journey: Two Lost Hours Aboard a Flying Saucer*, was published in book form and the Hills unwittingly became the subject of much unsolicited media and public attention.

Barney died young, at age forty-six, of a cerebral hemor-rhage in 1969. Betty quietly soldiered on, resolute in her belief of what had happened to them, despite the naysayers. In fact, as time passed, the mockery of those less than convinced of the Hills' claims quieted as numerous new groups, UFO researchers and enthusiasts, and the just plain curious sought out Betty for further details of their experiences.

She traveled widely, talking to groups and giving lectures, and was quite public about their life-altering incident. In 2004, after a struggle with cancer, Betty Hill died at age eighty-five. To the end, she never wavered in her conviction that their experi-ences were real, not fabricated for media attention. She argued that they were a quiet, civic-minded couple who had no interest in drawing attention to themselves. In fact, they were a biracial couple at a time when such marriages were still unusual.

They were active in their communities, were on a number of local boards of directors of civic programs, and Barney was appointed to the New Hampshire State Advisory Committee to the US Civil Rights Commission. He served on the local NAACP chapter and on its regional board, and they worked on Lyndon Johnson's presidential campaign to such a degree that they were invited to the inauguration in Washington, DC. So why, Betty contended, would they seek such a bizarre method of drawing attention to themselves?

Kathleen Marden, Betty Hill's niece and the executor of Betty's estate, has worked diligently for years to keep her aunt and uncle's story known to the public. She has curated the couple's impressive archives, consisting of eighty-seven folders including correspondence, personal journals, essays, manuscripts, magazine and newspaper clippings, photographs, slides, films, and audio tapes of their radio and television appearances. She also coauthored the fascinating and informative book *Captured! The Betty and Barney Hill UFO Encounter.*

Sadly, though acceptance comes slowly in cases such as the Hills', they lived in a state in which wily politicians know a good superlative when they see one. Much marketing hay has since been made of the fact that Betty and Barney Hill's Franconia Notch encounter is regarded as the first officially reported UFO abduction in the United States.

On July 20, 2011, the State of New Hampshire put its money where its mouth is and erected an official historical marker on Route 3 in North Lincoln, commemorating the momentous events of the night of September 19–20, 1961, a night the Hills were brave enough to discuss in public.

As far as the other "stars" of this story are concerned, the aliens themselves, we can only speculate as to how the information they gleaned from the Hills benefited them and their kind. It seems safe to assume that the Hills were neither the first nor the last humans abducted by space aliens for the purpose of edification of non-Earthlings. We may never know, or we may find out tomorrow, just what it is they learned and hope to learn from us. If the rate of occurrence of such incidences tells us anything, it's that our friends from beyond the stars are hardly meek and disinterested.

On the contrary, in New Hampshire alone we are regularly treated to accounts of UFO sightings through the state. But this is hardly a recent phenomenon: A number of intriguing unidentified flying objects, notably large gleaming discs and triangular-shaped crafts, have been photographed through the years swooping low over the mountains, highways, and river valleys of the Granite State.

Way back in 1870, for instance, what is widely presumed to be the oldest known photograph of an unidentified flying object was made at the summit of Mount Washington. The description accompanying the photo states: "Summit Mt. Washington Winter 1870–71." It is a stereo or 3D image, for the left and right eye, and is unusually clear, with decent detail. In it one can see a mass of clouds over Mount Washington and in the midst of them, a long, dark, cigar-like object. It has been examined numerous times by professionals and it cannot be easily explained away as anything other than an unidentified object.

The original image was auctioned on eBay in 2002 for $385. What makes it even more interesting is that at the time, in 1870, there were few flying objects in the skies, and there was no record of dirigibles over New England skies at the time, though steerable hot-air balloons had existed in Europe for a century.

A New Hampshire gas station has even gotten in on the alien abduction act. In Lincoln, at the Franconia Notch Irving

Express gas station, conveniently located on Route 3, on the Hills' route, there's a memorial to aliens and alien encounters. Outside, an original painting depicts an alien standing in the road, a UFO in the sky beyond, and trees and mountains all around. But it's inside the restroom that the real shrine to UFOlogy exists, for the walls are plastered with all manner of clippings, photos, and drawings relating to aliens, UFO sightings, and the possibilities of life from other planets visiting little ol' Earth, and specifically little ol' New Hampshire.

Indeed, UFOs are serious business in the Granite State. And why shouldn't they be? Especially when sightings keep on happening in the White Mountains. Take what has come to be known as the "Incident at Exeter." Not only was the 1960s the decade in which the Hills had their alien encounter, but in 1965, and again in September, the town of Exeter had its own encounter. On the morning of September 3, just after midnight, and just outside of town, eighteen-year-old Norman Muscarello was hitchhiking on Route 150, from Massachusetts back home.

All of a sudden, something big—roughly ninety feet in diameter—descended at a fast clip out of the sky toward him. It dipped and wobbled, noiseless, then retreated toward a nearby house, over which it hovered. It backed away, and when it did, the young man ran to the house and hammered on the door with his fists, but no one answered.

Soon a car happened by and the couple inside brought the frazzled young man to the police station. Muscarello convinced the officer on duty to send an officer back out there with him to see if they could spot whatever it was he had seen.

Not long before that, the officer they called back to the station had come across a young woman sitting in her car, too stunned to drive. When he'd asked what was the matter, she described the same thing Muscarello had seen.

Muscarello and the officer, Patrolman Bertrand, retraced the kid's route back out to Route 150. The clear, starry night was oddly quiet as the two men looked around the location where Muscarello had seen the huge flying craft. And then it appeared again. The kid saw it first, and the previously skeptical Patrolman Bertrand turned at the sound of the young man's voice.

"Oh my God," said Bertrand. The thing was massive, with lines of pulsing lights along the edge facing them, and it hovered, sometimes wobbling erratically, a mere one hundred feet above the ground. It appeared to emit a mass of bright red light over everything below it, and it moved toward the stunned young man. The officer, fearing radiation, snatched at Muscarello and dragged him back to the police cruiser.

Once inside the car, he grabbed the microphone. "My God," he shouted. "I see the damn thing myself!"

The two men sat there in the car, watching the UFO as it wobbled silently a hundred feet up over structures, landmarks, and a field. Frightened horses and barking dogs made the only sounds in the otherwise silent night. Then, with no warning, it flew slowly away, though on a seemingly directionless track, darting, turning, slowing, and then shooting off at another odd bearing.

Shortly, another sighting was called in by a young man who claimed to see a UFO, and his fantastic description matched those of the others. The Hill case and this series of up-close sightings shared the same documenter, author John G. Fuller. He ended up writing best-selling accounts of the Hills' experience (*The Interrupted Journey*) and of this one (*Incident at Exeter*).

Instead of doing their best to ignore the potentially strange looks and negative impact to their region and tourism dollars, the town of Exeter has embraced its UFO-related celebrity status. In August 2013 it celebrated its fifth annual Exeter UFO Festival, a one-day event filled with an interesting mix of fun and fact.

The Ossipee region, north of Exeter, along the eastern edge of the state, is also a long-known nexus of the inexplicable. In fact, New Hampshire's version of the Bermuda Triangle is called the Ossipee Triangle, and has been the scene of many strange events, tales of hauntings and weird crimes, sightings of odd creatures, and most notably, UFO encounters. A number of folks over the years have witnessed odd spacecraft plunging down into the allegedly bottomless depths of Snake Pond (formerly Mystery Pond), as well as into other local bodies of water, including Ossipee Lake, all rumored to be connected via underground caverns.

The region is considered sacred in Indian legend. In 1800 a burial ground was unearthed containing as many as 10,000 concentrically arranged remains. Some archaeologists claim it was the work of an ancient Celtic tribe.

Did aliens instigate these bizarre incidences or was the region already a nexus of strangeness, something to which the aliens may well be attracted? Since odd things continue to happen in the Ossipee Triangle, it's a safe bet we'll have more information to work with as time marches on.

As if to emphasize the strangeness that seems to envelop the Ossipee region, just south of there, but also in Carroll County, sits the solid town of Wakefield, tight to the Maine border. On the cold morning of January 10, 1977, a local farmer looked out his farmhouse window and noticed that despite the chilly temperature, there was a perfectly round, three-foot-wide hole punched through the almost dead center of the eighteen-inch-thick ice covering his farm pond. The farmer ambled on out there, poked a pole in the hole, and felt something down there. He squatted down for a closer look and saw what looked like a black boxlike object. A square something that had made a round hole, he thought. Hmm.

Local police were called, leading to more and higher-powered investigations, and reports of abnormally high counts of radioactivity were emitted from whatever was in his pond. Then the National Guard roped off the area. Throngs of gawkers gathered, airports far and wide were consulted—nope, no one had dropped a thing from any planes. But the next day the radiation was gone. And so was whatever the farmer had seen in his pond. Some of the gathered crowd were certain they had seen the National Guard remove the square object and then haul it off in a truck. Officials denied this and later claimed nothing had ever been in the pond.

Except that the farmer knew better. He'd seen something—and the hole didn't freeze over again. The circle in the ice is interesting, as is the report of radiation. Its shape is reminiscent of the series of circles on the trunk of Betty and Barney Hill's car, circles that for a time caused the needle on a compass to spin erratically.

The circle motif is also reminiscent of a wide singular round pattern impressed into a field in 1971 on yet another farm, this time in Walpole, in southwestern New Hampshire. It was investigated, and a number of folks referred to it as a "UFO nest." Who knows how many more such incidents have occurred? And how many were quelled by a government eager to cover it up?

Could it be that the US Air Force had been conducting tests with experimental spacecraft all along? They do have a base in Portsmouth, after all. Something tells us the answer is not so simple as all that.

CHAPTER 2

The Presence

Dweller at the Summit of Mount Washington

F or the summit of Mount Washington, official home of the world's worst weather, that June afternoon in 1996 had turned out to be rather mild. A college student, interning as an assistant at the Mount Washington Observatory, had decided to take a short hike alone to clear his mind and enjoy the fine afternoon. He had been hiking halfheartedly down the trail from the summit to the nearby hikers' hut when he felt there was someone behind him. He felt as if whoever it was held an arm outstretched and was about to tap him on the shoulder. He glanced behind, but the trail was empty.

He continued on, chuckling at himself for giving in to such silliness. He recalled the stories he had heard of other weather station employees' encounters with what they called "The Presence." At the time, he'd been far too busy learning his job to dwell on what he had dismissed as childish tall tales for the benefit of the new guy. Now he half-wished he'd paid more attention to them.

He'd almost reached the hut when a new and overwhelming compulsion to turn around gripped him. Someone was there, he now knew it. With the speed of a fingersnap, he felt his neck hairs bristle as bone-chilling terror tightened his gut and jellied his mind. He spun once more on the trail, his heart churning like a locomotive in his chest, and saw . . . nothing.

But it didn't stop him from wanting to scream. For there was something with him on the trail. Some *thing*, some *presence*—yes, they were right, that word was the best description of it—mere inches from him, of that he was convinced. It was neither beast nor man, yet both, too. Something not of this world, something *felt* rather than seen, something to be feared.

He had to run! He bolted down the trail, even though he knew what he thought was there simply could not be there. All logic defied it. He was alone on the trail, and yet he sensed something there, a presence. The Presence. The one everyone had joked about. Now he wished he'd paid attention. Had they mentioned something he could do to get away from it? Some trick, some sort of tried-and-true method of outrunning it?

As he ran for his life, his heart pounding harder in his chest than he could ever remember, he suddenly knew he had to run all the way down off the mountain, had to get out of there if he were to stand a chance of surviving. And then he knew the thing had drawn even closer. He felt his skin growing cold and clammy,

Native Americans have long referred to Mount Washington as Agiocochook, or "Home of the Great Spirit." Many people who work at the Mount Washington Observatory, at the summit (pictured), claim to share the space with a malevolent bodiless entity known only as "The Presence."

heard his breath stuttering, felt his lungs burning, craving what he could not give them, and he knew he wouldn't make it.

As the edges of his vision blurred, then pinched out to black, he wondered if his friends would ever find him—and if they did, what would be left?

* * *

At 6,288 feet above sea level, the summit of Mount Washington is the highest point in New England and all of the Northeast, and the most prominent mountain east of the Mississippi River. It's also one of the coldest places in the world. Winter temperatures at the cluster of ice-coated structures known as the Mount Washington Observatory often reach -70°F and colder in the winter months, given dips in wind-chill. At the height of summer, when outlet shoppers in flip-flops and shorts lick ice-cream cones and stroll the streets of nearby North Conway, folks at the summit can still feel spit-ting snow and freezing temperatures.

Mount Washington's summit is one windy spot. In fact, it was the official windiest place on earth for seventy-six years, based on a record set there on April 12, 1934, when a sus-tained gust of 231 miles per hour was recorded. And though the record was technically broken in Australia in 1996 by a gust from Cyclone Olivia (but not made official until 2010), folks the world over who know the import of such superlatives know the summit of Mount Washington still reigns as the windiest place on earth.

That's because in addition to such record-breaking blows, the summit regularly experiences an average of 110 days a year when hurricane-force winds are experienced. And yet since 1870, weather aficionados have endured extreme isolation, freakish cold, and nearly unendurable winds, all to bring the world its daily dose of weather. Crews of meteo-rologists, climatologists, and numerous other weather-related professionals monitor conditions and conduct experiments year-round at the summit's facilities—in buildings literally chained to the rocky summit, just in case a 300-mile-per-hour blow comes along.

As brutal as the place can be, the views from atop Mount Washington are also unparalleled: On a crystal-clear day, those lucky enough to stand at the summit can see much of 1,000 miles in all directions, including views into five states and well into the Canadian province of Quebec. Today's tourists can reach the summit on foot, via the Mount Washington Auto Road (since 1861), or by hitching a ride on the Mount Washington Cog Railway (since 1869).

Once it became obvious that the public wanted to reach the peak, nothing could stop them—or the number of hand-rubbing entrepreneurs who soon cut trails and a roadway up the mountain. In 1852 the Summit House was constructed, largely of stone, and became the first hotel at the peak, mere feet away from the very top of the mountain. Business that first year was brisk, to say the least, and another hotel, the Tip-Top House, was built the following year.

The two hotels served large numbers of visitors, impressive considering the only way to the summit at the time was on foot or on the back of a hardy nag. It had taken many such stout-hearted horses to transport the building materials for the hotels up nine miles of craggy pathways and cobby trails. By the turn of the twentieth century, the summit buildings included the two hotels, one of which housed a newspaper—*Among the Clouds*—and a weather observatory.

But in 1908 fire leveled all the summit buildings but the ninety-one-room Tip-Top House. And then, just as the Summit

House was rebuilt, the Tip-Top House was claimed by fire. It, too, was rebuilt and is still open to the public for tours as a state historic site.

* * *

In addition to extreme weather, there is another thing that many of the folks who live, work, and visit the summit of Mount Washington also endure. It is known as The Presence, and that's just what it is, an apt description of a powerful entity, a bodiless force that makes itself known primarily to people who are there for any length of time, though short-term visitors have also reported run-ins with this high-mountain mystery. But this being is no newcomer.

Before white Europeans landed on the shores of what they would come to call the New World, Native Americans lived in the region of Mount Washington, which they referred to as Agiocochook, or "Home of the Great Spirit." They were aware that something powerful yet indescribable dwelt atop the mountain.

In 1642, thirty-two-year-old Darby Field, a native Bostonian of Irish ancestry, and resident of Durham, New Hampshire, became known as a translator for the local Indian population. He was also an inveterate hiker, a man who liked to get out and about and stretch his legs. As with so many natural-born trekkers, something stirred deep within Field at the sight of the enormous white presence that is Mount Washington, and he decided he had to climb the "white hill" . . . just because it was there.

Of Field's 1642 ascent, Governor John Winthrop, of the Massachusetts Bay Colony, wrote in his journal: ". . . at the foot of the hill where was an Indian town of some 200 people. Some of them accompanied him within 8 miles of the top, but durst go no further, telling him that no Indian ever dared to go higher, and that he would die if he went. So they staid there till his return, and his two Indians took courage by his example and went with him."

Was it an irrational fear on the part of the residents of the Indian village, or did they know something the whites would only begin to comprehend hundreds of years later? There is no account of any unexpected chicanery experienced on the mountain by Field or his Indian friends, but as we will learn, that doesn't mean they weren't being watched. Just ask any number of hikers who have ascended the peak since—and come back down at a fast clip, trembling and looking over their shoulders.

* * *

To many hikers, bagging this massive peak is a major triumph. They arrive at the top under their own leg power, footsore, exhausted, dehydrated, and almost too wiped out to be elated. That, they figure, will come in due course. In the meantime, they do little more than eat a hasty meal and retire to a frigid sleeping bag, eager for sweet, rejuvenating sleep. But sometimes sleep is slow to come, or it's interrupted, or it doesn't come at all. Sometimes they never even make it to their sleeping bag. Sometimes they barely get unpacked before they realize they are not alone at the shuttered Lakes of the Clouds hut in midwinter.

When pressed for information, a number of summit workers, such as members of the WMTW Channel 8 transmitter crew, will admit there is most definitely something else "living" up there with them. Something not corporeal. They say it exists in shadows, in corners, something they call a "corner cat," a fleeting shape seen out of the corner of their eye. These reports could be easily pooh-poohed were it not for the many unexplained, bizarre occurrences a number of people have had—too many, as it happens, to dismiss them as figments of isolated and overactive imaginations. They also swear it's not so easily dismissed as a ghost. And so they refer to it as "The Presence."

What is it and why is it there? Neither of those questions is easily answered, though a number of run-ins with it have been documented over the years. Summit workers have described mysterious banging noises, doors opening and closing of their own accord, and the sound of heavy footsteps in empty sections of the buildings. Others have witnessed clothing being thrown and cups suddenly moving as if shoved by an unseen hand, or levitating and hovering for a few seconds. Still others have seen toilets flush of their own volition. They have also seen the elevator operating with a will of its own, its doors opening and closing as if someone were entering or exiting—yet no one walks on or off.

The Presence also has a nasty habit of violently shoving people without warning, from the front or from behind. When the shovee looks to see who could have treated them so harshly, no one is in sight.

One employee of the television station happened to be the only person in the facility one evening. He'd gone to bed and drifted off to sleep. Hours later, in the cold stillness of the middle of the night, he heard heavy footsteps in the hallway, as if someone large were trudging toward his room. Knowing he was alone in the place, he wondered who this could be—surely not an intruder? He mustered his courage and when he swung open the door and peered into the hallway, left then right, he saw nothing. He closed the door and climbed back in bed. No sooner had he done so than he heard the footsteps once again—closer than ever, and they were accompanied with heavy, labored breathing.

With a thudding heart, the man huddled lower into his covers as a wave of overwhelming, irrational fear washed over him. It was a fear beyond anything such odd sounds should have caused in him, and yet he could do nothing to stop it.

Fighting this dread with all his strength, he bolted once more from bed, and with trembling fingers twisted the door's feeble lock. As he turned to climb once more into bed, he heard new sounds, the distinct and utterly unnerving sounds of . . . a party. Laughter, music, people talking and laughing—as if a party had blossomed downstairs, in full swing. With his last shred of courage, the confused and frightened man unlocked his door, poked a head into the hallway, and he heard the party sounds, now even more distinctly.

He inched his way to the head of the stairs, still hearing the soiree's din, so he stiffened his resolve and slowly descended

29

the stairs to investigate. When he reached the bottom, the room appeared as it should—an empty, dark place inhabited by nothing but furniture. The quaking man didn't get any more sleep that night. Instead he spent the time packing and vowing to never again spend the night atop Mount Washington, alone or with a crew. And he never did.

Many people who've had experiences with The Presence swear they've almost seen it, that it always exists just out of sight, right around the next corner or close behind them on the trail, yet when they spin around, convinced they'll finally catch a glimpse of whoever or whatever it is that is stalking them, breathing on them, making their hair spike and their skin cold, it's simply not there. But the dread it brings, lingering and tangible, hangs in the mind and clings like a strange odor to the edges of everything at the summit.

Another man at the summit felt the overwhelming conviction that someone was in a small room with him, even though he could plainly see that he was alone. The feeling intensified within seconds and he soon became consumed with the urgency of fleeing for his life. He bolted from the room, shaking and white, convinced that not only had he *not* been alone, but that whatever had been with him would have caused him great harm had he stayed in there with it one moment longer.

There are others who have lived and worked seasonally and year-round at the summit, and they swear that if there was something menacing up there, it never bothered them. Anything that might be construed as an unknown entity could easily be explained as the result of a mind overstimulated by loneliness, tales of previous employees' alleged encounters, and perhaps gnawed at the edges by a little cabin fever.

If there is a method to the madness of The Presence, it seems to increase the frequency of its appearances and tirades just after a violent act occurs on the mountain's mighty slopes—and perhaps throughout the White Mountains as a whole. Given that accidents and untimely deaths occur regularly there, this means that The Presence is likely a busy entity, indeed.

In the past 125 years, an average of two people a year have died in the White Mountain range—usually hikers, climbers, skiers, snowshoers, and others who stray from the trail and become lost and disoriented. Sometimes they slip from a tight spot and tumble to their deaths, and their bodies are found much later—if at all.

The worst, and to date the single most tragic episode of violence resulting in sad and untimely deaths on Mount Washington, occurred on September 17, 1967, when a trainload of tourists riding on the famous Mount Washington Cog Railway experienced the worst accident in the railway's 145-year history. While descending the mountain, a switch had somehow mysteriously tripped to the wrong position. It caused Engine #3 to derail a mile below the summit, at Skyline switch. The engine gained a rocketing speed, compounded by the weight of the cars, before breaking free from the train and pitching off the track.

The coach full of eighty passengers continued hurtling downslope with no way of braking, then drove straight off the trestle and slid several hundred feet down a graveled slope before slamming into a boulder. Seventy-two people were injured, and eight people were killed. (Despite this unfortunate blemish, the railway has safely transported nearly five million passengers to the summit in all its long years of operation.)

Through human error or malicious intent, the cause of the moved Skyline switch has never been determined, though many people suspect the unseen lurking evil of The Presence. In the weeks and months following the wreck, an employee of the railroad, who lived at the summit's Tip-Top House, experienced a number of odd occurrences for which he could find no explanation, and could discern no guilty party. He ended up calling in the New Hampshire State Police. All manner of goods had been moved, furniture was rearranged, the cash register was tampered with, and more. The police investigated, but found no clues as to who—or what—would instigate such behavior. They returned with a police dog and once again they found nothing that might indicate foul play. The employee was questioned thoroughly, but he was a trusted sort and no blame of the odd disturbances was affixed to him.

More recently, on a particularly stormy winter evening at the weather observatory, a handful of men who worked there were all gathered together, talking and reading, and playing board games. The night was particularly cold and blowy, with brutal wind gusts that would render the heartiest soul a frozen corpse within minutes of exposure.

So when a hard pounding rattled the door, the men all snapped their heads upright and stared at each other, eyes wide in shock. Who could that be? And on such a night? Nothing could be alive out there—at least not for very long.

Finally one of the men worked the latches and tugged the door inward. And he saw no one. He looked out into the dark, blowing gloom, looked left and right, and finally looked down. There at his feet lay a heavy bronze plaque. A plaque they all knew to be permanently affixed to a stone base at Crawford Path, one mile from the summit. How did it get there? Again he looked, but saw no footprints in the blowing snow, no sign at all of anyone playing a prank on them. Yet it would have been impossible for the wind to have uprooted the large, heavy plaque and then somehow, miraculously, deposit it at the door-step of the observatory. Impossible, they all knew. And yet . . . it had happened.

The plaque was a marker memorializing hikers who had succumbed to exposure in a sudden and raging snow and sleet storm on June 30, 1900, on a climb up Mount Washington. The storm trapped two hikers but a mile from the Summit Hotel. All about them, the terrain became a slippery, blizzard-like place of freezing temperatures and ice-slick rocks.

The storm, an unexpected, brutal squall, lasted for three days. Finally searchers headed up the mountain to try to find out

how their friends, William Curtis, sixty-three, and Alan Ormsbee, twenty-nine, had fared at the top. Instead they found the frozen corpses of the two men. Curtis was discovered first, near the
spot where the famous Lakes of the Clouds hut now stands, built
a year later to help fatigued hikers caught in unexpected weather.
Not far ahead of him on the trail lay Alan Ormsbee.

The spot at which Curtis was found was later marked
with a heavy bronze plaque commemorating the men. It was
the same bronze plaque found years later during another such
violent storm, distributed somehow by an unseen hand. But
that wasn't the first time the plaque had been uprooted and
dropped elsewhere.

A number of times during such unexpected storms, the
plaque became mysteriously dislodged and ended up on the
doorstep of the Lakes of the Clouds hut. Each time, workers
would carry the plaque back to the boulder from whence it came
and reaffix it. And each time it would once more mysteriously
loosen and relocate itself, with no apparent human help. Eventually the traveling plaque got its wish—it was finally bolted inside
the hut and there the plaque has remained, apparently finally
pleased with its resting place.

The deaths of Curtis and Ormsbee are regarded by American Mountain Club (AMC) members and other hikers as a cautionary tale to be heard with respect, humility, and as a lesson
that the weather that high up is a fickle thing with a mind all its
own. Many hikers, when passing the sad spot at which the men

perished, offer a quiet word of thanks and say that such a tragic accident could happen to anyone.

Every once in a while, though, some wiseacre cracks a flippant joke about how the two New York hikers from 1900 should have known better, should perhaps have turned back when the storm first showed signs of life. And it is these smart alecks who suffer odd consequences for their know-it-all attitudes. Often they are shoved, and several have described being punched in the chest by an unseen hand, a force powerful enough to send them sprawling backward on the trail, gasping for breath and immediately regretful of their inconsiderate remarks.

The deaths of Curtis and Ormsbee were tragic, to be sure, but they were not the first to die in such a manner at or near the summit. Nor would they be the last. The first to hold that dubious distinction goes to a thirty-five-year-old British vacationer named Frederick Strickland. As the son of a member of British Parliament, young Freddie enjoyed many of life's finer indulgences, including being a graduate of Cambridge University and heir to grand estates. In October 1851 he showed up with a friend at the Notch House, a place of accommodation serving that region of the Presidential Range. The very next day, after hiring a local guide, he and his friend set out to climb the mountain via the Crawford Bridle Path. By the time they reached the summit of Mount Clinton (now Mount Pierce), thick, steady snow had begun to pile up, driven by a slicing wind. The guide, a local with vast knowledge of the potentially treacherous peaks, urged them to turn back. Strickland was having none of it. Despite their pleading, the privileged man left his guide and his friend behind.

The other Brit and the guide descended the mountain without bullheaded Freddle, expecting him to give up at any moment and follow them down. Not surprisingly, he failed to show up at the Notch House by the next morning, so a search party was formed. He was found dead two days later, frozen stiff, facedown in a mountain stream.

On September 14, 1855, eighteen-year-old Lizzie Bourne was also caught in a sudden storm and, after an eight-hour climb, perished but a few hundred yards from her destination, the Tip-Top House. Such tragedies seem only to inspire and exacerbate The Presence's ire.

Whatever "The Presence" is, it seems to be content to ply its unnerving trade above the treeline, where the increasingly stunted flora give way to a tundra climate, with no trees, but plenty of wind-stripped rock. This might well be an ideal place for an unseen and largely irate entity to scowl, stomp, and brood about being disturbed by humans. Or maybe it's just a big prankster with a strange sense of humor.

CHAPTER 3

Death Cheater

Dr. Tom Benton,
the Menace of Mount Moosilauke

Just one more wedged boot into the rough granite trail, one more push upward, one more rocky handhold pulling himself ever higher . . . and so, the young Dartmouth College student kept willing himself upward. He'd grown more tired than he'd expected to be at this point, but he wanted to reach the peak of Mount Moosilauke, then head back down before the September afternoon's dappled light failed him.

Turning around before he reached the peak was no option—his father had taught him to never give up. But why did he always have to take the most difficult paths to the top? Despite his best efforts to push away any thoughts of defeat, exhaustion nibbled at his ragged, muscle-sore edges. He should have waited for his friends, but he'd been impatient to get on the trail, said he'd meet up with them later.

Despite his urge to press on, he had to stop for a breather. He didn't dare sit and risk stiffening, though the rocks were tempting. He'd try that birch off to the right of the trail. Lean there for a few minutes to cool down, catch his breath, and sip a bit of water. He might even indulge in a bite of granola bar. It was his own recipe, something he liked to make for hiking.

He leaned his backside against the tree and bent forward, stretching his back and shoulders. This route, up Jobidunk Ravine, was one he'd not been up alone before. Back when he used to hike with friends more and less by himself, they had come up this way a couple of times to climb the headwall, which wasn't much farther up the trail. He wanted to make the top, since the views were stunning. But he wasn't there yet.

"And I won't get there dawdling," he thought, swigging a last gulp of water, and then repositioning the canteen on his belt. He pushed away from the tree and slipped the small, blue day pack from his shoulder. As he tugged on the zipper to get at his stash of granola squares, a slight movement to his left caught his eye. It was almost as if there was someone standing behind him, just out of sight.

A pang of fear bloomed in his gut even as instinct pulled his gaze behind him, but there was no one in sight. He saw only the rocky tumble he'd just scrambled up, the trees, more stunted and thinner the higher up he climbed. He wanted to laugh at his silliness. And yet, there had been something there, his mind told him, hadn't there?

A sudden shiver zipped down his spine, as if traced by the tip of a long, ice-cold fingernail, from neck to tailbone.

Not far away, a branch snapped, and with it every sound stopped—the cheerful cheeping of chickadees, the high-pitched, grating caw of blue jays, the rat-a-tat of woodpeckers—even the infrequent breeze had ceased whispering the turning leaves against each other.

The young man looked downtrail again, and was surprised to see how high up he had climbed, and how steep the trail was. But what struck him most of all was that where seconds before he had seen warming shafts of sunlight slanting through the trees, illuminating the rugged trail, he now saw long shadows, bleak stretched things that both beckoned and repelled him from the darkening woods. Woods that he suddenly dreaded, woods that he knew he would have to travel straight through the heart of to get back to the parking area. The parking area where hours before he'd rejoiced on finding it empty of cars.

Empty. The word echoed in his mind like a lone, dropped rock, cuffing off the bone-dry stones lining a long-empty well. And when it finally hit bottom—when he finally came back to his senses—he knew he had to get down off the mountain, had to get out of there, had to get away.

He also knew he couldn't take the same trail down that he'd taken up. But he couldn't cut left or right or he'd never find one of the more well-traveled trails. He knew he had to go up before he could go down. He also knew he had to calm himself. There was no way he could let this sudden and silly feeling overtake him and make him do something stupid. One bad move on this rocky track and he'd be lucky to get out of it with a snapped ankle, and probably end up with a whole lot worse.

No, he told himself. *You have to get a grip. Have to keep this frenzied feeling at bay. The best way to do that is to keep on with your plans to climb the rock face and reach the top, otherwise you'll always give up in life.* If his old man had taught him anything, it was perseverance. The young man forced himself to turn and stare hard at the encroaching gloom, to prove to himself that nothing was there. That it was all in his head.

He forced himself to move upward, once again, toward the peak. Within a minute, the familiar work of climbing calmed him, and he soon almost forgot his attack of fear. He even allowed himself a grim chuckle—what had he been thinking?

He'd nearly reached the point where the wind, no matter the time of year, sliced steady and chilled a sweaty climber. The last stretch of the trail had been particularly steep and difficult. He reached upward, convinced with each grope that he would gain the top, when, at chest height, a withered hand clawed out from a black gap in the rock.

For a fraction of a second, the hideous thing seemed poised there as if unsure what to do, as if it were watching him, and the image of it fixed in his mind forever. It was a long-fingered hand, that of a man, but with wrinkled, gray skin. The fingers were tipped with curved, yellowed nails like claws stained by long years of smoke, age, and grime. Then the hand drove outward and shoved him square in the chest.

The young collegian barely had time to utter a strangled cry as he pitched backward and tumbled, pinwheeling downslope, caroming from rock to boulder for more than a hundred feet. He finally snagged on a stunted tree, an unconscious, bleeding wreck.

"Hey!" A hand clapped onto the young man's shoulder. He screamed and spun around, his blanched face a mask of terror and confusion. One side sported congealing blood running from beneath sticky, matted hair. His eyes skittered back and forth, unable to focus on his two friends.

"Whoa, whoa, buddy, take it easy. We're just glad to see you're okay." The friends exchanged looks and then glanced back at their friend, whose breathing was forced and ragged, as if he had been running for hours. He acted as if he'd been chased by something he still seemed to think was after him.

They agreed they needed to get him down to the hospital in Hanover, and quick. As if on cue, the frenzied young man's legs wobbled and he pitched into a collapse. They caught him and lowered him to a sitting position.

"Can't let him get me, can't . . ."

"Who are you talking about?"

But he didn't respond, just kept looking about the darkening gloom of the forest.

"Where's your pack, man? Looks like you took quite a tumble. You had us worried."

"Have to get out of here, he's coming . . . he's everywhere!"

"Who? Who's up here? Look, we're here, you're okay now. But who are you talking about?"

For the first time since they'd found him, long minutes before, the ragged hiker focused his dilated eyes on one of his friends and said, "He pushed me and I fell. Then when I came to, he chased me."

"Who? Who pushed you?"

"The old man, long white hair, long black coat. He had gray skin . . ."

"What?" One of his friends smiled nervously and shook his head. "No, man, I'm telling you, you took a spill, that's all."

"The stories . . . Dr. Benton. . ." The injured man locked eyes with his friends again. "They're true." Then he passed out.

The rescuers looked at each other, then hurriedly hoisted the unconscious man between them and made their way down the last of the trail.

Neither of them dared mention that there was no sound in the forest, no squirrels rustling leaves, no birds cheeping, no breeze rasping through the trees. That late fall afternoon, the slopes of Mount Moosilauke were dead still.

* * *

The sleepy little New Hampshire town of Benton sits in the middle of the state at the foot of mighty 4,800-foot Mount Moosilauke. In 1840 the town gained its current name (from Coventry) in honor of Missouri senator Thomas Hart Benton, aka "Old Bullion," proponent of the nation's westward expansion policies. The mountain itself gained its name from Indian sources: "Moosi" meaning "bald," and "Auke" meaning "a place."

In the late eighteenth century, a young man named Thomas Benton—presumably a distant relative of Old Bullion—quickly drew attention by being a most impressive and altogether different young man than the rest of the local youth. Young Tom, as he was known, was gifted with a natural intelligence and curiosity that quickly outgrew the town's one-room schoolhouse. Soon he was taken under the wing of a wealthy judge in nearby Plymouth, who recognized the lad's burgeoning intellectual abilities and wished to see him attain all that his ample young mind was capable of.

In time, Tom wished to become a physician, but the world's top medical college was based in Heidelberg, Germany. Since it was such an expensive institution to attend, and since not even his generous benefactor, the judge, could afford to send Tom to Heidelberg, a plan was concocted whereby the residents of the rural region of his youth would all chip in and send Tom to Germany to study. And in return, upon his graduation, he would return to Benton as a newly trained—and much needed—doctor. This suited Tom, as he loved the community in which he grew up, and had little desire to live elsewhere. And that is exactly what happened.

At medical school, Tom proved himself once again to be a student among students, after first learning to speak German in order to pursue his studies. During his time there, he befriended an equally brilliant old professor who had mysteriously been snubbed by his colleagues many years before, though the reasons for this snubbing remained vague to Tom. While Tom was still a student there, the old professor passed away. But to Tom's surprise, he left the young man a bit of money and a few personal items, the most curious among them a locked chest. Many years later, the contents of this chest would affect Tom's life and the lives of many other people half a world away.

After four years studying abroad, the brilliant young man returned to New Hampshire and kept his part of the bargain. He was soon regarded as a top-shelf doctor and served his widespread patronage diligently. He fell in love with the daughter of a wealthy businessman and all seemed right in Tom Benton's world. And then, in 1816, his beloved fiancée died of typhoid fever, an affliction beyond even his brilliant ability to cure.

Tom Benton struggled for months, but slowly became more withdrawn, missed appointments with patients, ignored his personal hygiene, and seemed to age greatly in such a short time. Townsfolk attributed it to deep grieving, but over time his demeanor grew much worse. He backed away from everything and everyone he knew—he refused to see patients, gave up his practice, and vacated his home in town. With few possessions, among them a strange smattering of laboratory equipment and the curious trunk given to him by the disgraced professor, the grieving Tom Benton withdrew to an abandoned hovel on the flanks of Mount Moosilauke.

Even then, on his infrequent trips to town, he was approached by people desperate for his medical attention. He refused them all, rarely speaking, and never acknowledging those confused entreaties from people he used to call his friends. Within months he was regarded as a crack-minded hermit best avoided by all. No one had an inkling of the blasphemous undertakings the warped doctor had engaged in, deep in the woods of Moosilauke.

He soon turned fully inward and concentrated his substantial mental abilities on the vast and dense contents of the mysterious trunk—all manner of obscure manuscripts, old books, letters, scraps of ancient scrolls, and assorted papers. Each page was alleged to hold the clues that guided his old professor's lifelong quest, the very thing that had earned him disgrace and disfavor in the eyes of his fellows as a promising young doctor himself.

He had bequeathed the trunk's promises to young Tom Benton because he recognized in him a kindred spirit, one who might carry on his life's work—the pursuit of the secret of eternal life.

Because he felt he had been cheated of a lifetime of happiness with his lovely fiancée, Benton now plotted his revenge: He would cheat death. And that's just what he set about doing.

Soon, local farmers began complaining that their animals—sheep, cows, goats, horses—were turning up dead. Too many, as it turns out, and with no apparent afflictions other than a curious red welt with a puncture mark in the center, and always located behind the animals' left ears. Puzzling as it was, what happened next left locals alarmed. Throughout the river valley, corpses of newly dead people began disappearing, then turning up a few days later, dumped unceremoniously where they might be found. And all these bodies bore the same strange wound behind their left ears.

Following a few such gruesome discoveries, a search party ventured forth and, as part of their rounds, they passed by crazy Doc Benton's shack in the woods. But it looked abandoned. They worried that he, too, had fallen victim to the strange affliction. They kept an eye on his place, checking it for several days, but he never showed up.

Over the next few years, though, hunters caught glimpses of Benton walking the woods around Moosilauke. They all described him as having long white hair and wearing a long black cloak.

In 1825, on a November afternoon, a Benton woman working in her kitchen heard her young daughter scream. She bolted out the door and into the side yard in time to see a tall, lean figure dressed in black making off with her screaming child. The woman's husband took off after the fleet-footed child-snatcher while his wife ran for help. Soon a posse of men tracked the mysterious kidnapper into the woods, following tracks toward Little Tunnel Ravine, then on up the side of the mountain. The terrain grew difficult, and then dead-ended at the base of a cliff. Where could they have gotten to?

Then they heard a maniacal laugh from high above. Looking upward, the posse saw Old Doc Benton, skylined far above atop the cliff, laughing like a madman, holding the struggling young girl high above his head. Then he tossed the howling child down at them. Alas, they were unable to catch her.

But to a man, they swore it was Dr. Benton. Yet despite searching for months, they could not find him.

Years later, in 1860, two men commissioned a hotel, the Prospect House, to be built at Mount Moosilauke's summit. They had a difficult time finding a crew that would agree to work atop the mountain. Despite the intervening years, locals still caught sight of Dr. Benton now and again, striding the woods, his long black cape and long white hair trailing. He had never been caught, but there was enough residual fear in the air that people up and down the valley didn't dare tempt fate. Even if it was not readily voiced, they firmly believed that the evil doctor was some-how still alive—if not well—and roaming the region.

The builders finally reached a compromise of sorts with a crew of carpenters. It would take longer to get the job done, but the carpenters would only agree to build the hotel atop the mountain provided they were not required to stay the night. In fact, even though the new hotel's grand opening was attended by more than 1,000 people that following July 4, complete with a brass band and other entertainments, no one booked a room for the night. They all descended the carriage road before dark.

The builders eventually hired two out-of-work loggers to winter over in the hotel. They supplied them with food, drink, firewood, and a telegraph line for communication. All went well for a month, then a three-day snowstorm hit. Supplies ran low

POSTAL CARD BY *THE NEWS*

Years after Dr. Tom Benton was known to have inhabited the slopes of Mount Moosilauke, filching corpses from the local community, the Tip-Top House hotel was built at the summit. But for much of its first year, no one dared stay there for fear of a visit by the deathless doctor.

and the telegraph line went out. Finally, one of the men suited up and ventured outdoors to try to fix the line. After an agreed-upon twenty minutes had passed, the second logger headed out into the storm to find his friend. He found the man lying prone in the snow, not far from the hotel's door.

The second man dragged his unconscious friend back inside and tried to revive him before the fire. But the man was dead, which was puzzling because it didn't seem he had been exposed to the storm long enough to kill him. But the logger did find a puncture wound behind the dead man's left ear. He knew only too well the tales of Dr. Benton. His tracks, found the following day, indicate he dashed into the night. He was never seen again.

Shortly thereafter, renamed the Tip-Top House, the hotel became a going concern, and for years hosted well-heeled hikers and tourists out for a few draughts of bracing mountain air. Then one October day in 1942, four Dartmouth students out for a hike found the hotel to be nothing more than a smoking, burned ruin, with only the stone chimney still standing.

Over the years, a number of people have claimed to have seen Dr. Tom Benton, or something resembling the creature he became—a thin wraith dressed in black and trailing a mane of long white hair. Most frequently hikers staying at Ravine Lodge, a place of accommodation on the southeast side of Mount Moosilauke, claim to have seen him. Sometimes it's little more than a fleeting glimpse of something—a hand, perhaps? Or prints of a style of boot that hasn't been worn since the 1800s.

While reports of corpses—man or beast—bearing odd wounds behind their left ears have ceased, that doesn't mean that the good doctor, now well into his third century, isn't out there securing whatever form of sustenance he needs to continue his odd existence, caught in his ever-diminishing capacity as a creature who pursued and unearthed the secret to eternal life. But at what cost?

* * *

Graverobbing in old New England was a fairly common practice, particularly in the vicinity of universities training medical students. Considering that much of Mount Moosilauke, including Ravine Lodge, is owned by Dartmouth College, perhaps the story of Dr. Tom Benton is a long-polished attempt by old-time Dartmouth students to justify bodysnatching transgressions of long ago.

A case in point: In the early 1820s, Charles Knowlton, a student at the New Hampshire Medical Institute (now known as Dartmouth Medical School), was found guilty of stealing a freshly buried corpse for the purpose of dissection. He was fined $200 and spent two months in jail. Daddy paid his fine; Junior did the time. The industrious young man went on to graduate in 1824 from the Medical Department of Dartmouth College.

In an effort to prevent the bodies of recently deceased loved ones from being disinterred and used in various nefarious cadaverous experiments, family members often took turns sitting graveside to deter corpse thieves. Called "cemetery sitters," these folks performed their grim task long enough for the bodies to no longer be of use to the thieves.

In 1825 one New Hampshire family, so fearful of their recently departed family member's body being stolen, and so weary from being nearly assaulted at the cemetery while guarding his grave, gave up their solemn duty and secretly disinterred the man themselves. They brought him home and buried him beneath the family woodpile. After a sufficient amount of time, they reburied him in his proper grave. It appears they were correct to take such precautions—when they reopened his grave, a log they had placed within had somehow been turned over.

CHAPTER 4

Mysterious Stones

. . . and the Men Who "Discovered" Them

On a summer day in 1872, two men, hired to set fence posts on a plot of land near Lake Winnipesaukee in the town of Meredith, traded off shoveling and scooping dirt. As the day progressed, a line of loose-set posts began to emerge. One of the men wielded a steel pry bar, loosening tight-packed soil, rocks, and clay from the sides of the spade-skinned hole. Now that they were down several feet in the latest hole, he stopped to let the other man scoop out the loosened dirt with the dull-ended shovel.

Soon the hole was deep enough that the spade proved nearly useless, so the other man knelt and scooped with his callused hand. "Hold up there—'nother rock."

"She's bony soil, all right," said the standing man, grateful for a breather.

The other nodded as he pulled up the latest impediment to setting another post. And he lifted free a knob of clay—not uncommon for that region of New Hampshire. But there was something about it—it was on the heavy side, and a smudge of black rock showed through one thin spot of clay.

"What you got?" asked the first man running the shovel, leaning down. "Something injun?"

"Hunk of clay, but"—he wrinkled his nose and scratched at the slick gray knob—"dunno, it's different somehow than the other rocks."

"Yeah, well, save it for Mr. Ladd. You know how he is about funny stones and such. As for us, we got to get this fence set, or he'll likely be put out that we ain't further on than we are."

"Yeah, and he'll be along soon."

"Speak of the devil," mumbled the first man. He nodded at a thin, dapper man striding up. "Afternoon, Mr. Ladd. We was just talking about you."

"That's why my ears were burning," said Seneca Augustus Ladd, the Meredith-based merchant who'd hired them. He eyed their progress as he slipped off his suit coat and slung it over his shoulder. "Looks like you've unearthed quite a crop of rocks."

"That we have. 'Bout the only good use of 'em would be for a stone wall."

One of the men nodded toward a darkish lump on the ground, misshapen and bigger than a man's fist. "'Cept for that." He bent to retrieve it. "Just now pulled it out of this here hole."

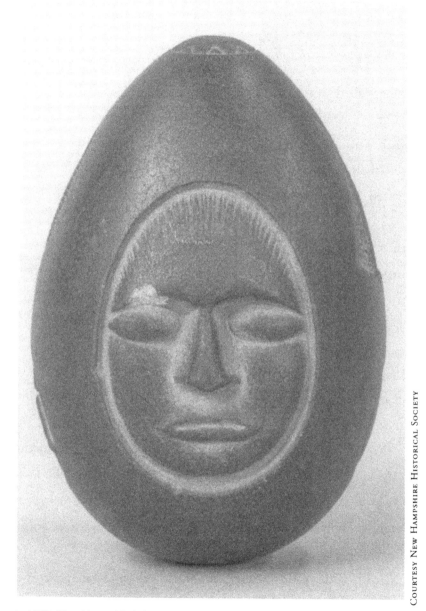

In 1872, New Hampshire's famous "Mystery Stone" was unearthed by workmen in Meredith while digging fence-post holes. The four-inch-tall, one-pound stone egg is highly decorated, of unknown origin, and the only one of its type in the world.

He nodded to their latest-dug effort. "Seemed odd, out of place. We know you like strange rocks and such, Mr. Ladd." He handed his boss the strange lump of clay.

Strange rocks, indeed, thought the merchant. What those rubes called strange, he called natural and man-made curiosities of great historic, geologic, and archaeological import. The merchant's near-scowl of disappointment at the slow pace of the work softened, transformed into a pursed lip, eyebrow squint as he hefted the strange clay-covered thing. "Where did you find this?"

"Oh, quite a few feet down in that hole there. You can see there's some sort of black rock inside the clay." The worker waited in vain for the boss man to acknowledge his comment, then shrugged. "We just thought since you're always collecting Indian arrowheads and such, that you might find that interesting."

As if a spell had been broken, Ladd said, "What? Oh, yes, thank you." He turned to leave them, thumbing away the drying clods of clay from the dark stone underneath. "Carry on setting those posts, men." But his mind was on the strange rock he held in his hand, a black stone that was rapidly emerging from the clay. For with each passing second as he smoothed away the flaking gray clay, he was sure that it was indeed some sort of Indian artifact. Perhaps it might be something to add to his collection! He half-smiled at himself. A man could hope. . . .

In truth, Ladd soon became aware that it was like nothing else he had seen in all his years as an amateur archaeologist. As a successful businessman, first as a maker of horse-drawn carriages and later of pianos and melodeons, and more recently as founder of Meredith Village Savings Bank, Ladd had the financial wherewithal to build up what he knew to be a sizable and impressive—and perhaps the largest—private collection of natural and Indian-made artifacts and relics in the state. But this, this . . . marvelous find! As more of the stone's details emerged, he suspected that he alone possessed something entirely precious and unmatched in his or, dare he speculate, any other such collection.

What emerged from its drying sheath of clay was a black, egg-shaped stone, large, perhaps the size of a turkey or goose egg, roughly four inches tall, and nearly two and a half inches across at the middle, its widest point. But the most striking features were the indentations that, upon careful inspection, revealed themselves to be impressively detailed relief carvings in the face of the smooth black rock.

One side sported a carved face, the largest of the carvings, which took up most of one side of the egg. It appeared to be a face in repose, perhaps of someone sleeping. The top of the stone was carved with a starlike pattern. There was little doubt that another of the carved symbols was a teepee, and the face could well represent an Indian face. There were also etchings of an ear of corn, arrow-like figures, what appeared to be a moon and stars, and several others that were less readily apparent and more difficult to distinguish as common symbols, such as an animal's leg (perhaps that of a deer), a bird or flying fish, and perhaps flames.

In the coming weeks and months, Ladd freely shared news of his discovery with whoever cared to listen—and he found that people were eager to learn about this strange, singular object. Beyond his own sharp curiosity, speculation began immediately as to what it might be, who might have carved it, and how old it was.

In November of that same year, 1872, Ladd was thrilled to have his find recognized in the pages of the publication the *American Naturalist*, the official journal of the American Society of Naturalists. In addition to a full accounting of the egg's discovery, the article went on to praise its possessor: "As Mr. Ladd is quite a naturalist, and has already an extensive private collection of relics and specimens, he was delighted with the new discovery, and exhibited and explained the really remarkable relic with an enthusiasm which only the genuine student can feel." The publication ventured guesses as to what the true meaning of the mysterious egg might be. It proffered the notion that it could be a symbolic token indicating "a treaty between two tribes" and called it "a remarkable Indian relic." That explanation seemed as likely as any that arose. After all, some of the symbols, such as the teepee and ear of corn, are logical for an Indian to have carved.

In time, as word spread about the strange, inexplicable discovery, the Smithsonian Institution approached Ladd about having a cast made of the stone so that it might explore the mystery on its own. He quietly denied such requests through the years. Perhaps Ladd was afraid of what they might learn about his beloved artifact. Other such denials of close inspection by scientific outlets fueled long-term speculation about Ladd's discovery.

He also rebuffed curiosity seekers and wealthy collectors of strange artifacts the world over who repeatedly offered to buy the stone. Could it be that he had been less than forthcoming about the mysterious egg's origins? It is possible that Seneca Augustus Ladd may have carved the egg himself, or hired someone to do so.

Perhaps Ladd had been inspired by the New Yorker who, just three years before, had hired a man to carve out of gypsum a statue of a ten-foot giant. He then buried it where it was "discovered" (conveniently on his brother-in-law's farm), in Cardiff, New York, and went on to make the con artist a fortune—despite the fact that the "Cardiff Giant," as it came to be called, was outed as a fake, and not the petrified corpse of a real giant from the deep, dark past.

Given that such a tale was fresh in the minds of the Northeast public, Ladd might have thought to have a little fun. As an established collector of various natural and man-made artifacts, he could have had access to such non-native materials. Perhaps then he planted it in a spot where he had instructed his hired men to dig fence-post holes.

It is also quite possible that the very man who possessed a vast collection of found artifacts might have been desperate to be remembered in the archaeological world for an important discovery. Such a find might land him in history books for years to come. If that were the case, then Ladd's elaborate ruse has likely exceeded his wildest dreams, for the inscrutability of the mystery stone endures today, 140-plus years after it was first unearthed, covered in clay, its curious markings slowly revealed for all to see.

Could Ladd have been that obsessed with gaining notoriety in archaeological circles? While that is possible, he never sought to profit from the egg. Giving him the benefit of the doubt, it is just as likely that he was merely a devoted collector afraid to learn, should the egg be scrutinized too carefully, that his exciting find did not live up to its mysterious promise.

For two decades, Seneca Augustus Ladd retained ownership of what came to be called the "Mystery Stone." In 1892, on her father's death, one of his daughters, Frances Ladd Coe, inherited the stone. She, too, kept it under lock and key, refusing to sell it, for a further thirty-five years. Finally, in 1927, she made a gift of the strange carved egg to the New Hampshire Historical Society, where it resides today, on permanent display at the society's Concord facility.

Given that no similar relic has been found anywhere else in the world, it has been speculated that the hefty egg may well be a prehistoric artifact; still others have hazarded guesses that it may be of Inuit or Celtic origin. The egg weighs in at a bit more than one pound, hefty for its size, suggesting a relatively dense composition.

But the most curious aspect of the mysterious paperweight may lie in what is *not* there—two holes, one in each end, that connect to form a neatly bored channel through the length of the egg. The hole at the top is ⅛ inch in diameter, while that at the bottom is ⅜ inches in diameter. And it is these holes that in 1994 raised the eyebrows of New Hampshire state archaeologist Richard Boisvert.

He performed a number of in-depth tests and analyses and determined that the end holes were far too regular in diameter and bored too smooth to have been worked by hand. Had the egg truly been an ancient relic, its holes should have possessed the uneven characteristics one would expect to find in a hand-hewn article of this sort. These determinations led him to the conclusion that the holes were likely caused by nineteenth-century machinery, specifically metal tools.

Furthermore, the archaeologist and his colleagues surmised that a number of scratches near the bottom of the egglike stone indicate that it was placed and re-placed on a metal shaft while the boring process was conducted. The testing also concluded that the stone is quartzite, a fine-grained derivative of sandstone or mylonite, of which no such specimens have yet been found in New Hampshire. State geologists have not ruled out the possibility that such a deposit may yet be found in the state, but so far . . . nada.

If the stone is of more recent manufacture, the state archaeologist's possible evidence lends credence to a past theory claiming that part of the reason the stone remained cloaked in mystery and unidentified may be that it belonged to a secret society, perhaps as an item used in a ritualistic service, not unlike those of the secretive Masons.

Yet another alternative explanation was proposed to the New Hampshire Historical Society in 1931. In an anonymous letter, the author offers the possibility that the carved egg is one of the world's mysterious "thunderstones," a physical manifestation of a folkloric belief that such artifacts as carved items and flint arrowheads and spearheads literally fell from the sky, fully formed. Given that in 1931 such items were still widely believed to exist—more so than today, at any rate—it is no wonder that the outlandish notion was given consideration.

Intrigue continues to surround the strange egg, despite—and perhaps because of—recent scientific attempts to explain it, explanations that have fallen short of being conclusive. And so we are left to wonder: How old is the stone? Who carved it? What was it used for—merely art, or was it intended for something more functional, such as part of a ceremony? Today's experts remain frustrated at the lack of information surrounding its discovery. The exact location at which the stone was unearthed has been lost to time and the advances of civilization. It is said the spot is somewhere beneath a parking lot in Meredith, preventing further digging in the region.

For now, those who believe the stone is an ancient, mysterious artifact brimming with potential undiscovered meaning continue to grapple with thin explanations that offer little more than speculation. To be fair, no one can decidedly disprove that the stone is an ancient totem, perhaps a key to a forgotten people or ritual. And until someone unearths a relic with comparable physical characteristics—to date no artifacts have been found bearing similar carvings and symbols—the true meaning of New Hampshire's Mystery Stone will remain a singular curiosity, as much for what we know about it as what we don't. Among believers, hope remains high that someone will discover its twin someday, shedding light on the true meaning of the mystery stone.

Until that day comes, it is possible for the curious to scrutinize it for themselves. New Hampshire's Mystery Stone, aka "the egg," is on long-term display at the museum of the New Hampshire Historical Society, 30 Park Street, in the capital city of Concord.

* * *

Speaking of misplaced rocks. . . . Though a few genuine Norse artifacts can be found in North America—among them items found at the L'Anse aux Meadows site in Newfoundland, and a Norwegian coin dating from the eleventh century found in Maine in 1957—there are many more alleged genuine Norse artifacts and locations that either cannot be proven legitimate or are considered outright balderdash. Among them are the three monuments in Boston to Leif Eriksson that signify the Viking warrior's purported trips to Beantown in AD 1000. Oh, the monuments are real, all right—it's the notion of Eriksson having toured the region that's in question. And then there's the fascinating Dighton Rock, located on the shore of Taunton River, in Berkley, Massachusetts, a massive boulder covered in strange symbols (Native American, Phoenician, Norse, and

Portuguese have all been theorized) that to date haven't been sufficiently deciphered.

There is also a stone tower in Newport, Rhode Island, and no one knows quite who built it, how old it is, or what it was intended for, though many claim it is of Norse origin. And who can forget the wonders of fabled Norumbega, the lost Norse colony, believed located at Narragansett, Rhode Island.

But New Hampshire is home to one of the most bizarre and controversial of Norse artifacts. We speak, of course, of the (in)famous Thorvald's Rock, located in Hampton, New Hampshire, a town also famous for being the hard-hearted home of the (alleged) witch Eunice "Goody" Cole.

Legend states that Thorvald (or Thorwald) Eriksson, brother of famed Viking explorer Leif Eriksson, headed a Norse expedition to the (rumored) Norse settlement known as Vinland, near Boston. Thorvald suffered a fatal wound in a skirmish with Indians, and as he lay dying, he requested that he be buried at the headland he called Krossanes. This spot is now known as Hampton, New Hampshire's Boar's Head promontory. Despite mentions of Thorvald's grave-marking stone dating back to the seventeenth century, when Hampton was established, the stone believed to be his marker, which sat at the end of modern-day Thorwald Avenue, is unlikely to actually be his gravestone.

A stone with multiple gouges and scratches, believed to be runic in origin, did reside there. But in 1989, largely because curious and greedy tourists had severely damaged it by chipping off chunks for souvenirs, the stone was moved to the grounds of the Tuck Museum. It now sits inside a stone-and-concrete enclosure with steel bars on top, in an attempt to keep people from further damaging the stone.

You may well ask: If it isn't Thorvald's Stone, what does it matter? In fact, scientists have studied the grooves and slashes—alleged runic inscriptions—in the face of the rock, believed to be poor Thorvald's epitaph, and have concluded that they are likely little more than glacial scratches, similar to those found on similar rocks nearby.

While it's largely accepted that Thorvald Eriksson died in the New World 1,000 years ago, it is believed that he is buried instead in eastern Canada, possibly in Newfoundland or at Cape Breton, Nova Scotia.

So how did all this Viking gravestone stuff come about in Hampton, anyway? We have one man to blame: Hampton district court judge Charles A. Lamprey, who grew up hearing of the mighty Thorvald. In due course, the local newspaper published an article he authored in which he claimed that a mysterious rock, conveniently sited on his land—land that he intended to develop into a beach cottage community—bore curious markings that he claimed the colonists referred to as Witch's Rock, and that Indians claimed sat atop the grave of a "white god." Hmm.

The story, despite a distinct lack of evidence, grew legs and traveled throughout the pages of a number of other newspapers. Soon the land was developed, its value greatly enhanced by the presence of a genuine Norse artifact—but not just any artifact. This one marked the grave of a Viking hero. The rock's home, Surfside Park, now sports a Thorvald Avenue and Viking Road.

Through the years the rock's legend became more famous and important than the rock itself, which at one time was shunted aside to make way for a sewer main. All the while, tourists pecked at it and toted off their ill-gotten souvenirs. Then a man from Massachusetts tried to haul off the entire rock one night in his truck. Various parties of archaeologists through the years dug here and there in vain for further proof that Vikings had done something—anything—in the Hampton region, but to no avail.

And in 1989, after all those years of fame, humility, and degradation, Thorvald's Rock—most likely just a big ol' rock—was moved to the grounds of the Tuck Museum, where today it resides in its protective enclosure. Visitors are most welcome at the Hampton Historical Society and Tuck Museum, located at Park Avenue, Hampton. But leave your hammer and chisel at home.

As for the man who elevated a few scraps of hand-me-down Viking legend into a full-bore duel with history and came out all the richer in real estate for it, Judge Lamprey is but one in a long line of Yankee hucksters who pulled a fast one, albeit with a chuckle, at the public's expense. But that doesn't mean the story isn't first rate!

CHAPTER 5

Stony Structures

Mysteries of the Granite State's Megaliths

The high priestess turned her stern gaze on the attendant dozen worshippers and, muttering strange sounds, held aloft a long, silver-bladed dagger. Sunlight slicing through the trees reflected off the weapon's jeweled gold hilt. Her murmuring grew louder, punctuated with random moans from the gathered acolytes, men and women, their swaying white robes now and again revealing the thing in their midst on which all their eyes were fixed. As the high priestess raised aloft the gleaming dagger, the devotees raised their arms in obeisance and leaned back, as if compelled by an unseen force. Thus was revealed the object of their attention, a nude young woman stretched out on a stone slab, not quite sleeping, not wholly awake. Flaxen hair cradled a head slowly lolling from side to side, her eyelids fluttered, revealing green eyes beneath, unfocused and unknowing what the strange scene about her portended.

Rising in unison, each voice of the worshippers and the priestess curled like rising smoke around others until they ululated in a crescendo of unholy hymn that drove the woodland creatures silent and compelled birds to take wing. The priestess' arms rose higher and higher, her robe's sleeves slipping to her shoulders. The dagger, clenched tight in her hands, pointed down, the tip glinting with menace.

The high priestess' eyes rolled back in her head, showing stark white orbs. Sweat ran down her cheeks. As if by unheard command, all the voices rose to an ear-ringing shriek, then stopped, and the dagger drove downward—

"Timmy . . . Timmy! Son, we have to get going. Come on."

Timmy McGraw jumped as his father's big hand gripped his shoulder. The boy shook his head and squeezed his eyes shut, then opened them wide.

"You okay, son?" Mr. McGraw squinted at the gawky thirteen-year-old.

"Yeah, I'm fine, Dad."

Satisfied with the answer, his father turned from the stone slab the tour group had been gathered around. He was eager to see the rest of the complex known as America's Stonehenge. But Timmy wasn't. He had no interest in seeing anything other than this slab. He'd read about it online and knew that some people, mostly scientists who just seemed old and dried up, anyway, didn't want to admit what he knew—that it really was a sacrificial altar. It had to be.

He looked around quickly, satisfied that no one else was nearby, and he held his breath as he reached out with a trembling right hand. His fingertips grazed the rough granite surface. Tenderly he trailed them inward, down into the shallow trough that lined the outer edge of the altar stone. He'd read that the groove had probably carried the blood of the sacrificed victims as it flowed to each side, hot and steaming, across the rock's surface, then down into troughs, and out the far end where the streams met and drained into a carved hole where it was gathered into a cistern . . . and then what?

He wasn't exactly sure, so he'd had to imagine it. Any further information he had found was scant. But they were here, finally, after begging his father for months to take him. They lived in Boston, so Salem, New Hampshire, wasn't that far north, just fifty miles up the highway. But they'd finally found the time. And now that he saw it with his own eyes, touched the cold stone, smelled the very air of the place, felt the presence of all those past sacrificed souls—it was almost too much to bear.

Did they really sacrifice beautiful virgins here on this altar? He didn't doubt it, could see it so vividly in his mind's eye. He stared down at the flat altar, bolder now, with both hands flat on the cold, unyielding stone. And he imagined it slick with the congealing blood of a victim.

"Tim! For the last time, will you get a move on? I swear, we came up here because of you, and now you're loitering. Aren't you even interested in this place?"

Tim turned wide eyes on his father. "Dad . . . do you . . . do you think they really sacrificed people here? Right here?" He pulled his hands from the stone as if it had suddenly grown hot.

His father came closer. "Tim, is that what this is about?" He put an arm around the boy's shoulder and steered him from the stone. "I read that it was most likely a place for the colonists to render lye from wood ashes, nothing more. There's no proof that any sacrificing of any sort ever took place here. Speculation, maybe, but no proof."

"But I read online that this site is thousands of years old, that maybe even Celtic monks lived here."

Mr. McGraw looked at his son in silence for a moment. Finally he said, "Looks like someone's been reading too much Robert E. Howard."

"Aw, Dad . . ."

Mr. McGraw winked. "Come on, let's see the rest of this place. It's fascinating, really." He smiled down at his son. "Even if they didn't sacrifice beautiful young women here."

Tim blushed, but as he walked away to explore the rest of what he was sure was an amazing place, he couldn't help looking back at the bulky, cold altar stone, keeper of so many secrets.

* * *

It is quite possible that America's Stonehenge is the largest megalithic site in North America. It's also as possible that it is not. Wait a minute, what was that again? Well, first things first: The term "megalith" has seen more of a generic use in recent years, but strictly speaking, megaliths are large stones used in the construction of architecture primarily in Western Europe in the second millennium BC. Nowadays the term "megalithic" has been stretched to include any stone constructions suspected of being of an advanced age. New England is home to a vast number of such ancient sites and structures—estimates of stone chambers alone exceed five hundred—in all manner of *deshabille,* not surprising considering their suspected age.

In 1826 while scouting for land on which to settle, farmer Jonathan Pattee came upon the spot we now know as America's Stonehenge. Given the fact that other such curious stony sites exist throughout New England and the Northeast, it is probable that the jumble of rocks wasn't so much a shock as an unexpected but welcome turn of events for Pattee. He recognized good value for his money.

During the eccentric Pattee's tenure there, it is likely he altered and added to the odd collection of rocks, passages, and chambers he found when he purchased the land. But the size and weight of many of the granite boulders and raw slabs of rock, some weighing as much as eleven tons, suggest they were in place long before his arrival.

As far as adding to the collection of stone contrivances, he did so in part to help hide and store kegs of cider. And as an abolitionist, Pattee and others of his acquaintance also used the site as part of the Underground Railroad to hide runaway slaves. Discoveries during excavations add proof to this guesswork:

Shackles, presumably pried from the ankles and wrists of slaves, were found on the site.

But its history predates America's Civil War era—by a long, long time. Just how long had the site been in use? Radiocarbon dating conducted on samples of firepit charcoal from the site revealed that the site had been in use for 4,000 years. And pottery shards found there date from 1000 BC. As for what it had been used for, many of the stones appear to be aligned with lunar and solar movement in mind. That reveals the possibility—or at least the tantalizing theory—that an ancient tribe of sun worshippers may have once used the site as a holy place of pilgrimage, perhaps as a stone calendar.

Unfortunately, it may remain forever a mystery in part because under Pattee's ownership in the nineteenth century, many of the stones from the sprawling thirty-acre site were drilled apart, sold, carted off, and repurposed by local municipalities as curbstones, foundation stones, fill, and for other uses.

It wasn't until 1958, when a man named Robert E. Stone (no kidding!) purchased the property that it came into its own as a for-profit tourist mecca. He instigated a substantial amount of retrofitting to the site, placing stones in secure spots, rebuilding structures, and shoring up chambers, pathways, and underground caverns. He also took many liberties with his reconstructions, ensuring that some of them matched up with his vision of what the place should look like.

In 1982 the current owners, the Stone family, changed the site's name from "Mystery Hill" (so named in 1937 by then-owner William Goodwin), which they believed promoted it as a less-than-serious roadside attraction. The new name, "America's Stonehenge," is an attempt to establish the site as a serious, albeit still mostly mysterious, archaeological attraction. Though in truth, America's Stonehenge appears to have more in common, structurally speaking, with Ireland's world-famous prehistoric monument, Newgrange.

The original Stonehenge and its wannabe American counterpart are both old, impressive stone constructions that were apparently built by ancient folks rippling with muscles, brimming with confidence, sporting impressive building techniques, and displaying a keen interest in astronomy.

Despite the charcoal and pottery findings, most archaeologists agree that the spot was not used for long-term habitation, rather for religious ceremonies by travelers, or perhaps as a pilgrimage destination and a locus of worship and celebration. It is doubtful that it was built by Indian tribes native to New England, as they were not known for using stone in their construction techniques.

The primary feature of the place, the central altar, or sacrificial stone, is a massive, 4.5-ton, rectangular stone table with a carved channel running around its perimeter. Many scientific skeptics maintain that the stone slab was never used for blood sacrifice, but erected, chiseled, and used by colonists in the production of lye, a primary ingredient of soap. It could also have been used as an apple pressing table, which goes along with Pattee's penchant for cider.

One of hundreds of ancient stone structures throughout New England, the town of Danville's "Beehive Hut" was lost to local legend until a few decades ago when it was discovered by children playing in the woods. As with structures at the vast complex in North Salem known as "America's Stonehenge," its age, purpose, and builders are unknown.

That said, just underneath the "Sacrificial Stone," an eight-foot-long channel leads to a small subterranean chamber that may or may not have been used by an old high priest as a way to unleash an otherworldly, domineering voice on the assembled worshippers high above. Or perhaps it was used to drain blood from an animal or, egad, human sacrifice? Too fanciful? Maybe that's the point, since no one has yet to say with any certainty just what the bizarre, sprawling complex is.

Despite the speculation and lack of definitive answers, Mystery Hill, aka America's Stonehenge, continues to hold a secure spot high on the list of North America's most intriguing and unexplained places. In fact, only one thing about America's Stonehenge is certain—no one knows quite what it is. But it is open to the public, year-round, at 105 Haverhill Road, in North Salem. Perhaps you will be the one who cracks the mystery.

* * *

As amazing as America's Stonehenge is, it is not alone. There are hundreds of megalithic sites throughout New England. Many are little more than a single simple stone structure, cairn, or standing stone, perhaps signifying a long-ago site of sun worship. Others are more complex and feature ample evidence of artfully planned out mounds, dolmens, and underground chambers.

One of the more impressive, albeit more demure than the structures at Mystery Hill, resides in nearby Danville. This small town's stony contribution to this list is a handsome specimen known locally as "The Beehive Hut," though it's not beehive-shaped in the least. It's a man-made stone enclosure consisting of two massive slabs for its roof (roughly six feet long, six inches thick, and five feet wide) set atop well-placed boulders fitted together to form the walls of this modest structure.

Butted up against a hillside, the opening faces southeast. Roughly three feet tall by less than two feet wide, the chamber inside isn't much bigger than that, with a depth of three feet or so. It's just big enough, it's said, for two people to huddle inside, as long as they refrain from getting too boisterous. Structurally it is similar to a number of other such stone huts found throughout New England, and as with many of them, its history is mysterious. Its builders are unknown, as is the date of its construction, and the very purpose behind its construction.

The shelter had been known locally, but in legend only. Then, several decades ago, local boys playing in the thick woods found it, lending immediate credence to the legend. One story says it was used as shelter for men put ashore to trap and hunt. Another speculates that the hut is one of a number of such shelters marking a southbound trail used by shepherds driving flocks from the north of New Hampshire to market in Boston. And of course, a number of people through the years claim it bears astrological significance. One thing's for certain—it seems that where ancient stone structures of New England are concerned, there's always room for further speculation.

But that hasn't stopped folks local to Danville from taking pride in it. The Danville Heritage Commission has taken care in recent years to preserve its mystery hut, and erected a brass marker nearby, which reads: "Beehive Hut: Unknown age and origin, similar to structures at America's Stonehenge, Salem NH."

Danville's Beehive Hut is located on public land and can be visited, but as the town requests, it is a prized historic site, so they ask visitors to please treat it with respect. To see Danville's Beehive Hut up close and personal, venture onto the marked path in the town-owned woods to the right of the town maintenance garage off Hersey Road, about two-tenths of a mile from Main Street (Route 111A). Or ask a Danvillian.

* * *

Though the stones at America's Stonehenge have been significantly altered throughout its history, at its most foundational level various constructions at the site are old—very old. But for pure archaeological value, the New Hampshire site that has offered diggers the most bang for their buck no longer exists.

The Neville Site, an archaeological site on the east bank of the Merrimack River in Manchester, is considered one of the most important archaeological finds in the entire Northeast. Occupied from 8000 to 5900 BP (Before Present) during the Middle Archaic period, and used by Native Americans for 8,000 years, the site was established by early foragers due to its prime location on the river. It provided a boon of fish, a relatively easy source of food to a people who had to expend much effort and energy searching far and wide for sustenance.

The Neville site, named after the owner of the property, John Neville, was not excavated until 1967, when construction of a new bridge posed a threat to what had up to then been considered a site of minor archaeological interest. One of the volunteer professionals working the dig, Peter McLane, took it upon himself to expand his dig area, delving deeper than was expected of him. And it was his curiosity that unearthed some of the oldest artifacts found in New England at the time—tool fragments dated via charcoal sampling to be 5,385 years old.

Since some of the artifacts found there include projectile points that share characteristics with others discovered farther down the Atlantic Coast, archaeologists believe the foragers who used the Neville site engaged in trade and cultural relations with people much farther south than originally believed.

Despite the archaeological significance of the Neville site in informing historians of the Middle Archaic period in the Northeast, construction of the bridge went ahead and the site was destroyed.

CHAPTER 6

Crazy Killers and Unsolved Deaths

The Curious Murder of Dr. Dean . . . and Other Heinous Homicides

New Hampshire's most notorious—and most intriguing—murder case took place nearly a century ago in the lovely little town of Jaffrey, at the base of Mount Monadnock in southwestern New Hampshire. The brutal 1918 killing of Dr. William K. Dean has inspired books, plays, poems, and movies; brought in the FBI; involved potential foreign plots; and divided Jaffrey's 2,000 residents into factions.

All this took place during World War I's dismal height, at a time when many were prone to believe that the "enemy" could well be one's own neighbors. The very idea that German spies bent on sabotage could be in their midst, especially for a town not all that far from the ocean, was within the realm of possibility to the residents of Jaffrey.

Used to working into the wee hours, sixty-three-year-old Dr. William K. Dean rose late on that particularly hot August 13, 1918. He checked on his wife, Mary, three years his senior, who had become increasingly infirm over the previous few years. Her level of coherence had slipped and her speech had become muddled. Dean had married her in 1880, although she was his first cousin (they had elected, perhaps wisely, to not have children).

Dean himself was regarded in town with mild curiosity. Born in Delaware, he spent his formative years abroad as the son of one of the first American missionaries to China, and as a youth was friends with the crown prince of Siam. Oddly enough, though he earned his degree, he never practiced medicine. His own health was always poor, and because he and his wife each brought moderate family wealth to their marriage, he could afford instead to be a gentleman farmer, indulging his pastoral pastimes.

That evening, he decided to head into Jaffrey to run a few errands. On his way back through town he met up with the sister-in-law of his longtime friend, town banker Charles Rich. Dr. Dean gave her a ride to Rich's house, where they found the banker relaxing with a compress held to his left eye, nursing a wound he said he'd just received from his horse, who'd lashed out, grazing the man.

Dr. Dean spent a pleasant hour at the Riches' home before heading back to his place at 10 p.m. He would never be seen alive in town again.

PHOTOGRAPH COLLAGE BY JENNIFER SMITH-MAYO

The grisly 1918 killing of Dr. William K. Dean, of Jaffrey, is one of the state's most notorious unsolved murders, and includes German spies, mysterious lights, and a body dumped in a well. The collage above shows a number of items the victim wore during his untimely demise by garroting, including socks and sneakers, the ropes and sacking that bound him, the horse blanket in which his head was swaddled, and the barn in which he was bludgeoned—as well as the calendar on which his addled wife wrote "Billie die" on the date of his murder.

Back home, he checked in on his wife, snacked on raisin buns, and then told Mary that since it was 11:30, he was headed to the barn to milk his cow. He asked her to please have a hot meal for him when he returned at midnight.

Mary prepared his meal and waited for him, sitting in her chair facing the window, as she always did, watching for his lamp light's return. Eventually she fell asleep. In the morning, when she saw that her "Billie" still hadn't returned to the house, Mary Dean telephoned a neighbor, asking him to come over.

A number of people arrived, including their friends, the Riches, in time to see Mary Dean walking toward them from the barn, saying, "Billie is dead" in a matter-of-fact demeanor. She followed that jarring declaration with an even more inscrutable one: "He is in deep water."

A quick search of the barn showed the gathering crowd that Dr. Dean was most likely missing and that he had probably been hurt—or at least someone had. Blood spattered the stable walls and floor. But where was the doctor? It didn't take long for someone to notice that a few hundred yards up the hill sat a covered water cistern. They slid off the wooden cover, poked and prodded in the dark depths with a pole, and felt something of substance down there. Soon the searchers were able to grapple onto the object with ice tongs and retrieve what they had feared—the body of Dr. William Dean, which had been stewing in six feet of water.

He was still clad in his canvas, rubber-soled sneakers, his knee-height black socks, and a pair of shorts. That was all that was visible of his body. From the waist up he had been covered in a burlap sack. This had been tied tight with the same rope someone had used to bind his hands and feet. When the sacking was cut away, they found Dr. Dean's head swaddled with a horse blanket tied tight around his neck. Also in the sacking had been a twenty-seven-pound stone, perhaps taken from the barn's foundation. The rock presumably was used to weight the body to sink it in the cistern.

When the horsehair blanket was peeled away, it revealed that Dr. Dean had been caught by surprise, bludgeoned by something blunt—perhaps the rock—then gagged, and garroted, resulting in a severe and deep wound that had caused strangulation. Naturally enough, local law enforcement sent for assistance, and over the next few days, all manner of officers and officials swarmed the farm for anything resembling a clue. But they found very little for their efforts.

Nonetheless, the attorney general began establishing motives and building potential cases against suspects. But as his office delved deeper, they found that there were numerous possible suspects. Chief among them was the strange Mary Dean.

She had been seen by a doctor prior to the incident, and he had deemed her to be of such a delicate disposition that she was practically unable to climb stairs. Yet on the day of the murder she was seen by all to be walking about the place with no trouble. She was thought by people who knew her to be jealous of what she had said in the past was her husband's overly friendly manner with other women. And then there was her mention of Dr. Dean being "in deep water." It was also speculated that through the window facing the barn, she may have seen the perpetrator dump Dr. Dean's body into the cistern.

Further investigation into the murder revealed more curious clues and possible directions. Dr. Dean had been renting a house to a Lawrence and Margaret Colfelt, who were of German origin. Also, folks claimed to have seen strange lights flashing from nearby mountaintops, including Pack Monadnock and Mount Monadnock, all visible from Boston harbor, seventy miles away, perhaps signaling in code to Germany submarines. Similar flashing lights had also been seen emanating from the house the Colfelts rented from Dr. Dean.

Since this was 1918 and the apex of America's involvement in World War I, suspicion naturally fell on the Germans. It was surmised that Dr. Dean had learned something of possible spies and had been killed because of it. Soon federal agents appeared in quiet little Jaffrey, questioning all about mysterious lights and the possible spies in their midst.

It turns out that some of the alleged light sightings could easily be attributed to stars twinkling high up in the sky. Seen through trees they looked not unlike lights being flashed in a seemingly random pattern, perhaps even a code. Alternately, other lights seen could just as easily have been automobile headlights traveling roads at night at a distance. This sentiment was shared by a number of Jaffrey residents, who felt that the notion of German spies signaling from atop the local mountains was absurd and represented little more than paranoia induced by the war.

Still others claimed there had been a group of fun-seeking local youths who regularly roved the region at night, looking for places to party. Perhaps Dr. Dean had found them on his way home, and they decided to confront him in his barn, a confrontation that turned violent.

Another suspect was Dean's friend, the banker Charles Rich. His scratched face and blackened eye, which he had attributed to a horse kick, could only be corroborated by his own family members, Dr. Dean being the other person he'd allegedly told. Perhaps an argument had settled on the two of them the previous evening. Perhaps the banker had been so incensed that he felt compelled to trail after Dean and confront him, only to have his rage get the better of him, resulting in the murder of the doctor while he milked his cow.

In searching the barn for clues, investigators turned up a three-prong cultivator that they believed had been used in some capacity in the crime. It is also interesting to note that Rich's facial wounds from the alleged horse kick somewhat resembled the marks he might have sustained had he been struck in the face with a three-prong cultivator. None of these various bits of evidence were strong enough to implicate Rich, and he was never charged with the crime.

If the murder had been premeditated—which is likely the case—whoever killed him had been familiar with his habit of tending his barn chores so late in the day. It is also interesting to note that his milk pail was never found. Perhaps the killer was thirsty and took the fresh milk with him?

But Dr. Dean hadn't gone to town the evening before merely to attend to errands. While there, he had confided in a Mrs. Morison, who he knew was headed to Boston the next day. He told her he had certain information that he claimed was too dangerous for a woman to know, but he asked her to tell authorities in Boston that he needed to see them urgently. He said that he had needed to be sure of his information, but that he was certain now.

And it is this bit of information that gives the most solid direction as to why Dean was murdered. Because he was a gentleman farmer who kept his own odd hours, he was awake when these alleged spies were conducting their signaling using white, red, and blue lights, blinking at odd intervals.

Since the late-owl Dean had seen these lights for some time, he had become increasingly convinced this was evidence of German spies. He felt sure they were using local mountaintops to signal to their own kind, hidden offshore in submarines many miles away, probably informing others about troop and supply movements. Dean had for some time tried to warn his fellow Jaffrey-ites but to (seemingly) no avail.

Though the Rindge Historical Society, in the nearby village of Rindge, holds in its collection a sleigh and a horsehair coat owned by Dr. Dean, it is the Jaffrey Historical Society that possesses the true treasure trove of artifacts pertaining to Dr. William Dean's murder. Among the fascinating finds are bags containing the very hemp ropes that bound his hands, feet, and head, the horse blanket in which he was wrapped, the canvas sneakers he was wearing at the time, his socks (with evidence of darning!), even a calendar from his kitchen on which his wife had written "Billie die" on the very date of his death.

Mary had a potential motive for murdering—or having her husband murdered—in the form of suspicion of his alleged roving eyes. So it is curious that she wrote "Billie die" on the calendar in present tense on the very day on which he was killed. One can't help wondering if she knew more than she was saying. And if she wrote it before or after his death.

A grand jury convened from April 11 to 19, 1919, but despite so much circumstantial evidence, they were unable to bring a single person to justice for the crime. And so the mysterious and gruesome murder of Dr. William Dean remains unsolved to this day, the only such unsolved crime in the history of Jaffrey.

Though the jury's still out, so to speak, on the Dr. William Dean case, it hasn't stopped a number of people from trying to make sense of the cold-case trail of stale breadcrumbs that leads to the edge of that deep, rock-lined cistern. To this day, descendants of the various parties accused and involved in the crime still hold definite opinions. Not surprisingly, one side feels the wife was guilty; the other feels the banker was the likely culprit.

So, was Dr. Dean's death the result of German spies, jealousy, or something else? Only a very few folks, perhaps only one—the killer—ever knew who killed Dr. William K. Dean . . . and they're not talking—they're dead. However, Dr. Dean's ghost is said to haunt the halls of the very fine Monadnock Inn, believed to be the favorite drinking spot of both Dr. Dean and his cohorts . . . possible German spies!

* * *

Where, oh where did Martin Ahern go? That's just what the family and friends of this Keene resident were asking themselves for more than a month in the late winter and early spring of 1869. After he'd been missing for a short time, they posted an advertisement on March 25 in local newspapers that read: "Information wanted: of Martin Ahern, an Irishman, about 40 years old, well-built, straight, full, red face, and weighing about 175 lbs. Any information concerning him will be thankfully received by his family."

It would be another month before they found him. But instead of bringing answers, his reappearance only raised more questions.

As an Irish immigrant, Ahern arrived in Keene in 1861, worked for the Cheshire Railroad, and eventually established himself in a home he built on Island Street. On the evening of March 20, 1869, Ahern and a number of friends topped off a day of woodcutting at a friend's house, that of Thomas Boyd. Their big meal was followed by indulgence in copious libation and a rambunctious sing-along until the wee hours. At 2 a.m. the party broke up and the men weaved their way back to their own homes. They all made it back, save Martin Ahern.

A few hours later, the early-morning railroad watchman caught sight of something strange under a bridge nearby the Faulkner and Colony Mill. He investigated and found Ahern's sawhorse, saw, and hat, but found no man to which they belonged. Throngs of men searched the river, and the surrounding region, but Ahern was nowhere to be found. Finally, the local law decided to sink spikes along the canal downriver in hopes that if Ahern had drowned, his body would snag there.

In the interim, the police questioned numerous people, but turned up no useful information. It wasn't until April 28 that answers—and then more questions—emerged, along with Martin Ahern's body, which caught on the spikes that had been driven into the canal just for him. An investigation by coroner Samuel Woodward determined that Ahern's skull had been bashed in, likely through intentional violence.

It is possible, though doubtful, that the body had somehow been overlooked in the riverside search for Ahern. It was widely believed that whoever had killed Martin Ahern had waited what he or she felt was a decent cooling-off period, then had hauled the body out of hiding and floated it down to the waiting canal spikes where it would be discovered.

Though robbery was the suspected motive, and perhaps nothing more than a knock to the head of a drunken man had been the perpetrator's intention, the result had been far worse. The truth is unlikely to ever be known—the crime remains unsolved to this day.

* * *

One of the most frustrating feelings in a law enforcement officer's life is realizing that the case he or she has worked on for months or perhaps years is unlikely to ever be solved. Magnify that feeling by hundreds of individuals, public and private, over decades of dedicated and dogged pursuit of clues, of chasing down seemingly irrelevant tidbits of information, and you have the beginnings of the widespread frustration still felt up and down the vast Connecticut River Valley, the riverine cleft dividing Vermont from New Hampshire.

The great source of frustration is that the crimes—a series of murders possibly committed by the same person—remain officially unsolved. To date there have been seven official homicides in the Claremont, New Hampshire, region and throughout the wider Connecticut River Valley attributed to an unknown murderer. Unofficially, there have been eleven total killings in this region linked by shared patterns, such as similar sites at which the bodies were dumped, geographic proximity to each other, and the fact that the bodies bore evidence of multiple stab wounds.

The first of these unsolved but possibly linked murders took place in 1968, when a fourteen-year-old girl was sexually assaulted and strangled in Charlestown, New Hampshire. The last such case involved another fourteen-year-old girl who disappeared in 1989. Her remains were found in New Boston, New Hampshire, in 1991. In between these tragic bookends lie at least nine other lives taken by one or more killers.

The public's attention was first brought to bear on the possibility of a serial killer in its midst beginning in the mid-1980s, when three young women from the Claremont, New Hampshire, region vanished. In 1985 the remains of one of the women were discovered. Then a thirty-six-year-old woman was savagely stabbed to death in her home in Saxtons River. In 1986 a second body was found, one of the original three women who had disappeared. And shortly thereafter, the body of another missing woman was found.

Soon police investigators turned their attention to past cases to try to discern similarities—and they found two that had taken place in 1978 and 1981. At this point, their worst fears and suspicions were confirmed. It seemed likely that there was a serial killer on the loose in the otherwise quiet Connecticut River Valley. In March, 1987, another woman's body was found.

Then in 1988 a woman, seven months pregnant, was assaulted in West Swanzey, in a convenience store parking lot. Her attacker stabbed her twenty-seven times and left her to die. The woman, however, managed to climb back into her car and drive toward a friend's house. It was then she realized that her attacker, whom she had seen driving a Jeep Wagoneer, was driving ahead of her on the road. She managed to get to her friend's house, where she received help, but saw the Jeep turn around and drive by slowly. Both the victim and her unborn baby survived, though the victim suffered a severed jugular vein, collapsed lungs, lacerations to her kidney, and other serious wounds. She was able to provide the police with enough information for a composite sketch and partial identification of her attacker's license plate.

Despite this information, they were unable to make any arrests. After the last attack, the killings appear to have ceased. The reasons for this may be that the killer himself has died. One of the men unofficial investigators consider a primary suspect died in 2005 in Florida in a murder-suicide, having shot his estranged wife and his stepdaughter, and then himself. Though he had a number of strong coincidences that aligned him with several of the Connecticut River Valley killings—he owned a Jeep Wagoneer, and he had been in New Hampshire at the time when several of the killings took place—to date no physical or circumstantial evidence has been considered compelling enough to link him to the crimes.

Another suspect had confessed to a brutal rape and stabbing death of a twenty-six-year-old woman in Vermont, but later recanted his confession and was acquitted. However, he has lived in the three towns in Vermont and New Hampshire where most of the murders were centered. He has also been imprisoned on charges of lewd and lascivious conduct with a child. He was released from prison in 2010 and, as with the other suspect, cannot be officially linked to the Connecticut River Valley killings due to lack of compelling evidence.

And so to date, the notorious, nefarious, and brutal crimes of the Connecticut River Valley Killer remain unsolved, forming a terrible wound not allowed to heal, and standing in stark contrast to this otherwise bucolic, picture-book region of New England.

* * *

On a dark, stormy, and freezing night during the unusually brutal winter of 1817, a destitute artist stumbled up to the bleak, windswept home of farmer Peirce and his wife. He offered to paint murals on the walls of their front room for them in exchange for room and board. Though they had little, they agreed and he proved a most suitable hired hand to the farmer. In the evenings, the artist, who kept to himself and spoke little of his past, retired to the parlor to work on his murals. Then one morning, they discovered the man had simply vanished. He left behind his few meager possessions—art supplies—and stunning full-wall murals throughout the room, but of his whereabouts, they never learned.

In searching their parlor for signs of the vanished man, they discovered hidden panels flanking the fireplace, and a dark passage beyond. Surmising it had been built by Peirce's grandfather as a means of escape should Indians attack, the farmer followed the tunnel as far as he was able—it led toward the family's graveyard, some distance from the house. But there the trail dead-ended, the tunnel having collapsed some time before. Still the astounded farmer found no sign of their missing artist, and returned to the safety of his home and wife.

Eventually two men, detectives from Boston, traced the artist to the old Peirce farm. They explained that the man they had known as John Smith had fled thinking he had killed another man in a fight over a woman. The injured man, however, had not died, and they felt compelled to find the mistaken artist.

A year to the night following the midwinter visit by the artist, the farmer and his wife sat before the fireplace, reading and chatting, much as they had a year prior. Then a strange sound emanated throughout the room. It sounded as if it were coming from just outside, as if someone were scratching at the windows. They sat still and listened. As the wind gusted and buffeted the house, they then heard footsteps crunching in the snow outside, as if someone were walking around the house.

The farmer lit a lantern and swung the door wide, staring into the swirling gloom. But he saw no one. He ventured farther out into the snowy night. From the doorway his wife soon heard a shrill scream.

She ran into the night and found her husband stretched out prone on the snow, a terrified grin pulling his mouth wide. His eyes were saucered, reflecting a deep, agonizing fear. His breath came in short pulls, thready and raspy. She gripped his face and screamed for him to respond, but he could not. Finally she dragged him toward the house, hastily rigged up their horse, and managed to get the man into the wagon. By the time she got him to the local doctor's house, her husband was dead. The doctor drove her home and searched the dooryard for footprints of the person who had lured her husband outdoors. But he only found tracks belonging to the farmer and his wife.

The story has all the makings of a ghost story. Except that the farmer and his wife did live there, and he had died inexplicably and in the manner depicted. And the artist really did live with them for a time. In fact, there is a single photograph extant of one portion of the murals. The image, taken in 1937 after the house had long been abandoned, is of poor quality, but serves to further support the existence of the murals, the artist, and of the story itself.

The house itself no longer exists, and the family graveyard is a largely forgotten tumbledown of stones. The mystery of the Old Rindge House's curious artist remains as mysterious and unsolved today as it ever was—and no doubt ever will be.

CHAPTER 7

Pirate Gold, Pirate Ghosts

Buried Treasures of the Isles of Shoals

S hould you find yourself at New Hampshire's southern end, head east from Rye for six miles and you'll be (a) wet and (b) among a cluster of wind-chafed islets known as the Isles of Shoals, just off the New Hampshire coast. The nine rocky little knobs—Appledore, Smuttynose, Duck, Star, White, Cedar, Lunging, Malaga, and Seavey—vary in size, but total roughly six hundred acres in all. Although five of the nine islands belong to the state of Maine, most New Hampshirites claim the entire cluster as their own, whether the states decree it or not. In fact, when people speak of the islands, they generally refer to them as "those islands off the coast of Portsmouth, New Hampshire."

The largest, Star Island, is a tree-free zone, mostly rock, but it sports a hotel, a church, and even a cemetery, proving that there really is enough soil there to bury the dead (though how deep?).

Photograph courtesy Library of Congress

Pirate treasure is said to abound along the rocky shorelines of the nine islands that make up the Isles of Shoals, such as the Gorge on Appledore Island (above). The Shoals were a favorite retreat for buccaneers looking to bury loot and lay low.

Seals can often be seen sunbathing on the rocks near the tideline, and pods of porpoises regularly course by, dallying over unseen fish runs. Speaking of the region's oldest industry, though the waters here are still considered prime fishing grounds, they were at one time decidedly and prolifically excellent.

In fact, that's what they were named after: shoals, or schools of fish, that drew fishing ships from all over the world. Captain John Smith, in 1614, was the first to go public about the amazing and bountiful sea harvests hereabouts, though the impressive fishing grounds were well known to locals prior to his "discovery."

While they plied the local waters, European fishermen benefited from the relative protection the islands provided from the tribes of sometimes-hostile Indians on the mainland. The whites' ample catches, hauled and dried on a series of great racks called "flakes," capitalized on Europeans' fondness for dried cod.

By the time the mid-1800s rolled in, city folks south of the New Hampshire coast, in Boston and New York, cast their eyes northward, especially in summer, in an effort to escape the stifling heat of the overcrowded urban centers. Grand hotels began appearing inland as well as up and down the New Hampshire and Maine coastlines, including on the Isles of Shoals. Among these, massive hotels were built on Appledore and Star Islands. The latter is now owned by a private church-based foundation, which packs the island and its various structures all summer long with conference-goers, who still seek the same thing people did here 150-plus years ago—respite from the heat and the hustle and bustle of congested city life.

But how many of those summercators know that the waters surrounding the islands are a-jumble with wrecked galleons and pirate ships, many still concealing vast riches in cargo? And that despite those suspected, albeit waterlogged, riches, more pirate and non-pirate treasure has been discovered on the sandy beaches and wedged in the rocks of the Isles of Shoals than has been pulled from the surrounding brine?

* * *

It is said that the infamous pirate Blackbeard, aka Edward Teach, was a six-foot, six-inch brute with a waist-length beard, and that he wore a cutlass and twin flintlock pistols wedged in his belt. He is also rumored to have had fourteen brides (three of whom he murdered) in his short, action-filled life. At the time of his death in 1718, he left behind forty children. If that's true, it's a wonder the man didn't die of exhaustion instead of meeting his bloody end at sea. One of those wives—who may instead have been a mere girlfriend—the sixth of the lot, was a pretty young thing named Martha Herring, with whom he set up housekeeping on Star Island.

But hold that cutlass . . . another version of this oft-told and oft-conflicting tale says that Martha Herring was the young bride of one of Blackbeard's protégés, a young sailor named Sandy Gordon, who had incidentally led a mutiny aboard Ms. Herring's father's ship, the *Porpoise*. Having been caught by her father, British Captain John Herring, in a compromising position with his teenage daughter, Gordon received seventy-two lashes, which nearly killed the young, love-struck fool. When Gordon recovered, he struck back by tying the Captain, his future wife's father, to the mast and lashing him to death.

He ended up leading the crew of the *Porpoise* on a pirating rampage, plundering English vessels off the Scottish coast. But he grew greedy and refused to share the loot with the men who'd been loyal to him. So they put him and the girl ashore on a small Scottish island. Months later, pirates came ashore for water and it was then that Gordon met and impressed Blackbeard. Enough so that the "Terror of the Sea," as Blackbeard was called, soon gave him command of a captured French ship. It was this ship, renamed the *Flying Scot* by Blackbeard, that carried Gordon and crew, now laden with loot, to the Isles of Shoals to bury their booty.

Blackbeard dallied there long enough to replenish his ship's stores, and to make a deposit in what had become quite a popular bank of sorts among the piratical-minded set. With a handful of his subordinates, Teach buried a significant stash of ill-gotten loot, distributed, it is said, between Smuttynose and Londoner (now Lunging) Islands.

"Bury it deep, curse your foul souls!" growled the dread pirate Captain Blackbeard to several of his men laboring under his watchful gaze. Up and down, up and down, their implements rose and fell, breaching an ever-deepening hole in the bony soil. . . .

Another version of the story states that he buried part of the treasure, consisting of bars of pure silver and coins of gold, on the beach that now faces Star Island Hotel, halfway across the beach. Yet another nugget handed down through the years claims the treasure is buried just below the waterline, east of the Smuttynose breakwater. If any of this is true, Blackbeard never blabbed. He purportedly only ever said of his money: "Nobody but the devil and myself knows where my treasure is."

One fine day, while his crew lazed about, fat, happy, and sated with ample food and drink and sundry other amusements paid for with their ill-gotten loot, one of the men spotted a British man-o'-war ship.

While his men scurried about readying their gear and dipping oar to get to their own ship, moored in the island's harbor, Blackbeard smooched his wife, patted her rump, and warned her in no uncertain terms to never ever reveal the location of his treasure to anyone, no matter the threats they might use against her. And with that he left his wife there, alone on Star (or Smuttynose!), vowing to return for her as soon as the British danger had passed. He made his way to his ship, a grim smile playing his beard-hidden lips, while his young wife wept and waved from shore.

Perhaps he left her there to help stand guard over his treasure? Perhaps, as was his wont, he'd grown weary of her company and used the sudden presence of the British navy warship as an ideal excuse to once more take to the high seas to pursue his thieving ways? We may never know. But one thing is for certain—he never did return for his wife. Blackbeard left her there, living a lonely, solitary life, which is what she did for roughly two decades, until she died in 1735, still waiting for her beloved bold pirate. But she didn't leave.

Legend states—and numerous treasure-hunting eyewitnesses swear to it—that the ghost of Blackbeard's young wife still roams the shoreline of White Island, her inky black cloak snapping in an unseen sea breeze and her long, golden hair waving in the wind as she stares out to sea, waiting for a fearsome lover who will never return.

Legend also states a slightly different variation on the story. The alternative version involves our young newlywed Sandy

Gordon, who having bid Blackbeard adieu weeks before, had been enjoying time with his new bride, when they spotted a British man-o'-war. He knew he had to engage them, so he rallied his crew, kissed his wife, said he'd be back shortly after he disposed of the irksome British vessel, and rowed out to the waiting *Flying Scot*. Alas, the man-o'-war readied sooner, firing a volley of cannon shots that sank Gordon's ship, and he went down with it, leaving Martha Gordon, née Herring, to fend for herself, alone on White Island until her death in 1735.

That there was a Ms. Herring/Gordon/Teach is little questioned, and that she died alone and pining for her love until her lonely end is also historically noted. That her ghost has been seen numerous times is also accepted, gazing out to sea, bereft of hope, her long hair, dress, and shawl whipping in the wind, her woeful cries riding the breeze for miles around.

The intriguing but twisted tales of Blackbeard's life have left many people scratching their heads for many years about just what happened. The only thing that really matters, however, is the one that begs the all-important question: Gordon's wife or Blackbeard's, pirate treasure was apparently buried there. So why hasn't anyone dug it up yet?

* * *

Blackbeard's booty is hardly the only suspected loot buried or lost near the Isles of Shoals. The wrecks of many wayward sunken craft riddle the cobbled bottom around the cluster of islands.

A Spanish ship, the 400-ton galleon *Conception*, wrecked on Cedar Island Ledge one night in a ferocious storm in 1813, just off Smuttynose Island. At the time, the one person who lived on Smuttynose, Sam Haley, found only fourteen bodies of the twenty-eight crew members who had been aboard. No one survived, but for ten days following the storm, a mass of splintered timbers and jumbled cargo washed ashore on the little islands, including oranges, raisins, clothing, and a handful of silver coins.

Three years later, Sam Haley's son, Sam Jr., was busily constructing a seawall connecting Smuttynose with Cedar Island and discovered four bars of pure silver wedged under rocks on the south beach of Smuttynose. Though many people attribute this find as being some of Blackbeard's fabled stash, a number of historians agree that the bars probably came from the wrecked *Conception*. Haley didn't particularly care where they came from—he sold them for $4,000, a veritable fortune in 1816.

In 1685, a Spanish galleon wrecked near the northside cliffs of Star Island, and though her offerings of coins were slow in surfacing, her immediate contributions came in the form of timber—the salvaged wreck was used on Star Island to build a church, part of which still stands today.

* * *

Following Captain Kidd's Boston capture in 1699 and extradition to England the following year, where he was tried, hanged, then gibbeted on the Thames River—his rotting corpse serving as a warning to all who might have had designs on taking up the life of a pirate—his supposed first mate, Phillip Babb, settled for a time on Appledore Island. As a pirate himself, Babb was well off financially and had a house built there. During its construction, he instructed a crew to undertake an impressive excavation at the head of the cove, not far from his house.

Oscar Laighton, New Hampshire historian, wrote: "The pit he made was thirty feet across and ten feet deep, as I remember it, but the place was filled up level in the great storm of 1851." It was suspected that Babb had been acting on the promise of what he'd considered reliable information about the location of a treasure, most likely that of his old employer, Captain Kidd. Given that the mighty storm quashed his efforts, and that the US Coast Guard, in the early years of the twentieth century, erected a boathouse on the very spot where Babb had pursued his fruitless quest, it seems unlikely that the spot had, or will yield, pirate booty.

Babb, of course, is famous also for allegedly being the pirate responsible for the fascinating New Hampshire saga of Ocean-Born Mary (though that depends largely on which account one considers the "true" version of the Ocean-Born Mary saga).

But it is Phillip Babb with whom we are most concerned at this point, precisely because he never left Appledore Island. To this day, visitors to the island are stunned to see his apparently harmless ghost as it roves the rocks, spectral coattails flapping in the ever-present breeze. It is said his shade is so common that he is considered a mere local.

He is forever doomed to protect in death the very treasure he could not find in life, a cache said to top out at $100,000, yet to be claimed. And if Phillip Babb has anything to say about it, it never will be.

But what could be more evocative of piratical activity than unearthing a clay pot brimming with sixty Spanish silver coins? That's just what happened in 1870 to one lucky beachcomber, who then worked diligently, though ultimately unsuccessfully, to locate yet more buried stash.

While Blackbeard might win the blue ribbon for most memorable of pirates to ply his trade in and around the Isles of Shoals, it is Captain John Quelch who is said to have buried $100,000 in silver and gold somewhere in the Shoals. In the summer of 1703, Quelch first began his short-lived career as a pirate aboard the eighty-eight-ton privateer brigantine *Charles*, on which he served as first officer. As part of a mutinous crew that tossed overboard their sick—but not yet dead—captain, Quelch was elected leader by his fellow mutineers. From Massachusetts they headed toward South America and by the following March, Quelch and his men had unleashed ruthless pirate fury on no fewer than seventeen ships.

They headed northward once again and encountered a Spanish ship along the way that he claimed had foundered, so naturally they relieved her of her gold and silver as well. Then they slipped back into port at Marblehead. But before they did so, they paid a visit to the Isles of Shoals, anchored in Gosport

Harbor, and buried at least two hundred silver bars on Appledore Island's west side, though folks in Marblehead, Massachusetts, still claim that the copious amount of loot was buried not far from their own town docks. Still others claim he buried it at Snake Island, off Marblehead. No doubt the debate will continue until someone unearths the silver lode. But Quelch was not quite finished with the Shoals.

Captured the day after their arrival, Quelch and his men were jailed in Boston. In short order, and in true pirate form, Quelch led an uprising and he and a small crew escaped. The fugitive buccaneers made their way to Salem harbor, where they stole a boat and sailed, post-haste, the twenty-two miles to the Isles of Shoals. Unfortunately for them, the law was not far behind and they were caught holding the bag on Star Island—in the form of a great quantity of sacks of stolen gold dust. Oops!

All told, twenty-five of the forty-three *Charles* crewmembers—including Captain Quelch—were captured, and though they argued that they were merely poor, misunderstood privateers and not pirates, their pleas fell on deaf ears. Seven of them, again including the hapless Quelch, were tried, convicted, and on June 30, 1704, hanged in Boston's Scarlett Wharf as pirates. A big crowd cheered as their necks snapped like carrots. Quelch and two others were cut down the next day, their bodies chained and cuffed, and they were gibbeted on a small island in Boston Harbor called Nix's Mate where, for years, their decaying bodies swung in cages as reminders of the unfortunate effects of piracy.

When Quelch died, he took with him information on the whereabouts of a substantial buried stash of ill-gotten goods. Rumored to consist of significant amounts of silver bars, gold and silver coins, gold dust, and gems, all secreted in and among the Isles of Shoals, Quelch's retirement fund was forever lost, for his loot remains unfound to this day.

If there's a moral to the loot-riddled history of the Isles of Shoals, perhaps it is that a tourist looking to get out of the city and relax on a wind-swept isle off the coast of New Hampshire would do well to make room in his luggage for a metal detector and a shovel.

CHAPTER 8

Witches of the Whites

The Hard Lives of "Goody" Cole, Granny Hicks, and the Walford Women

Eunice Cole, also known as "Goody," short for "Goodwife," a common appellation given to the matriarch of a household in the sixteenth and seventeenth centuries, forever holds the distinction of being the only woman ever convicted of witchcraft in the state of New Hampshire.

In 1656, a healthy four decades before those wacky folks in Salem, Massachusetts, began accusing everything that seemed peculiar of witchcraft, poor Goody Cole, of Hampton, New Hampshire, was accused of cursing cattle. She was convicted and sentenced to life behind bars. Apparently feeling that a witch's powers were somehow not sufficient to help her escape, her fellow townsfolk sent her packing to prison in Boston.

How did this old crone earn such enormous community enmity? For starters, her neighbors regarded her as a surly old thing,

PHOTOGRAPH BY JENNIFER SMITH-MAYO

To mark its 300th annual town meeting, in March, 1938, Hampton, New Hampshire, feted Eunice "Goody" Cole and restored her citizenship—the very town that in her life had reviled her for alleged witchcraft.

hard to get along with and crabby. Some even said she was revengeful and filled with malice. Despite the fact that we all have traits that others find odious, surely these are not reason enough to ruin someone's life. And yet that's just what the good folks of Hampton did. Poor Goody lived at a time when superstition, paranoia, and accusation were the order of the day. Anyone with a modicum of sense might have guessed that berating one's neighbors and being generally argumentative might get them unwanted attention, but if this occurred to Eunice, she never let on.

Goody was an easy target, one of those people others just love to pick on, probably because they were guaranteed an amusing outcome once the old wet hen began cackling. And goad her on they did—even children got in on the act. Two young boys once crept up to her house and peeked in the window. And what do you think they saw? Why, as luck would have it, they witnessed Goody Cole and the devil himself—in the guise of a red-hatted black dwarf—colluding over a pot of tea and a plate of cookies. The tots claimed to have witnessed Goody arguing with her houseguest. They ran home and related all they had seen. Oddly enough, no one saw fit to ask them what they were doing creeping about Cole's home.

Soon other folks chimed in, claiming that they, too, had witnessed peculiarities with the old stick. One neighbor stated in court that Goody had threatened him. And the result? Two of his cows up and died. Goody also apparently told a neighbor that if his calves strayed onto her property and grazed, she hoped the grass poisoned them, or at least that the creatures choked to death. And lo, it came to pass that one of the calves did indeed expire.

Another tale relates how Goody claimed that while she was no witch, she knew of one in Hampton, a witch who had transformed a man into an ape. And come to think on it, claimed Goody, the child of one of her neighbors looked an awful lot like that ape. On and on the stories, threats, and curses volleyed back and forth between Goody and her incensed neighbors. No one liked her and she liked no one, but really, she should have kept her mouth shut.

Another child, a little girl this time, claimed she heard Goody's voice speaking to her through various creatures, including an eagle, a cat, and a dog, all attempting to lure her into Goody's house. Still two other Hampton women, Mercy Sleeper and Sobriety Moulton, claimed that whenever either of them uttered aloud the name Eunice "Goody" Cole, a frequent occurrence, given that they spent a good deal of time talking about the old crone, they heard strange scraping sounds at the window. Naturally, they attributed these sounds to Goody.

Based on such flimsy evidence and lopsided accusations, Eunice "Goody" Cole was imprisoned three times in her life for witchcraft. The first was a relatively short sentence, a warning shot of sorts that she failed to heed. Then in 1656, when she was in her seventies, Goody was publicly flogged and sentenced to life in prison. In 1662 she petitioned the court to let her out to care for her ailing eighty-eight-year-old husband, William. Her request was denied. Soon her husband died, and the town appropriated her land, home, and possessions to help cover the cost of housing Goody in her dank Boston jail cell. She served fifteen years and attested to her innocence the entire time.

In 1671 her case was finally reheard and the judge agreed to set her free, but covered his backside by issuing a public statement saying that there was still just cause of "vehement" suspicion of her continued familiarity with the devil (a catch-all way of claiming someone is acting witchy).

By the time Goody made it back to Hampton, she was in poor health, penniless, and alone, reliant on begrudgingly given charity of the people of Hampton. The next year, in 1672, she was once again arraigned on charges of witchcraft. She spent a number of months in jail until her case came up in April 1673. She was not convicted this time and was once again set free.

Now well into her eighties and with nowhere else to go, Goody was forced to live alone, shunned by all, in a rough little hut near the center of Hampton. As she was quite aged, she could no longer care for herself. Town officials assigned a different Hampton family each week to supply the "bewitched woman" with food and fuel, or pay four shillings to cover the cost of such expenses.

This went on for some time, until one day someone noticed that the food left on Goody's doorstep had gone unclaimed and no smoke rose from her chimney. Ding-dong, the witch was dead—but the townsfolk were far from finished with her.

A number of accounts document what happened next with Goody. None of them do any credit to those long-ago residents of Hampton. One version states that a group of surly citizens flung her corpse off a cliff into the sea. Still another claims they buried her, without a Christian ceremony, on land that had once belonged to her and her husband. But the most enduring version is also the most lurid, and the one that has stuck like a hard-cast spell to the legend of Eunice "Goody" Cole. A mob of townsfolk, on finding the bewitched woman dead, dragged her from her hovel, tossed her body into a roadside ditch, drove a wooden stake into her heart, and hung a horseshoe atop the stake as alleged protection from her certain postmortem wrath.

By now, the true story of what happened to her body has been lost to time and buried beneath layers of collective shame of ye olde Hampton.

Sadly, what it boiled down to in the end was that although Eunice and her enfeebled (and much older) husband were poor, they did own a choice forty-acre parcel of land at the town center. Given that she was prone to provocation, she made an easy target for those who would have her land.

Nothing says, "Sorry to have treated you so poorly," like a homely, wrinkle-ridden stone. But that's just the memorial Goody Cole has ended up with on the grounds of Hampton's Tuck Museum. In addition to the lumpy, unmarked rock, placed there in 1963, nearly three hundred years after she was accused of witchery, in 1938, a gaggle of guilt-wracked Hamptonites formed "The Society in Hampton for the Apprehension of Those Falsely Accusing Eunice 'Goody' Cole of Having Familiarity with the Devil." The group's intention was to exonerate the only woman to ever have been convicted of witchcraft in the Granite State. From a marketing standpoint, it worked—in spades. The group's efforts were so successful, in fact, one has to wonder if it wasn't merely a clever marketing campaign disguised as altruism.

At Hampton's three-hundredth town meeting, on March 8, 1938, townsfolk passed a resolution to restore Goody's citizenship to the town. That was just a warm-up. For the main course, they publicly burned certified copies of the official court documents of conviction, mixed the ashes with soil from the spot where they thought she may have been dragged and dumped, along with a dollop of soil from the site of her Hampton home. These ingredients made their way into an urn, and the citizens of Hampton vowed to erect a marker in her honor and bury the ceremonial urn beneath it. Alas, in all the ensuing media hubbub, somehow the urn was, ahem, misplaced. When found, years later, it was presented to the Tuck Museum and can be viewed there today. Still very much unburied.

But the 1938 restoration gambit caused quite a media storm: The story was picked up locally, and then reinterpreted numerous times throughout newspapers all over the United States, including the *Boston Sunday Post*, the *St. Louis Post Dispatch*, and *American Weekly*. NBC dramatized Goody's tale and blasted her alleged heresies through radios nationwide. Eunice "Goody" Cole became a household name, a pop star before the world knew of such a thing.

On August 25, 1938, Hampton held its memorial service, broadcast live from coast to coast.

Nowadays, Goody Cole is the town of Hampton's most famous resident, living or dead. The Tuck Museum has an exhibit dedicated to her. In fact, before it was the Tuck Memorial

Museum, it was the Frank Fogg House. And the Fogg family claimed that since the house sits on land once owned and occupied by Goody Cole, she is the reason they had no end of bad luck and no beginning of good luck while living there. They claimed that she haunted the place, causing their livestock to act queerly, with pigs and cows not doing whatever Fogg wished they would do.

Goody Cole's incredible, unfortunate life has spawned a number of books, poems, movies, and plays, not all of which are sympathetic, but most of which are entertaining. One of the most famous, a poem by John Greenleaf Whittier, is called "The Wreck of Rivermouth," and in it he blames the witch for the drownings at sea of several Hampton residents.

Undaunted, Goody's ghost has been seen at various times through the years roaming the roads in and around Hampton, sometimes scrutinizing the stones in local cemeteries, and even conversing with residents. She always seems keenly interested in the location of her memorial, and often goes away disgruntled with the fact that there's still no marker for her in Hampton.

* * *

"Goody" Cole was hardly New Hampshire's only person persecuted for alleged witchcraft. Granny Hicks, of New Hampton, nearing the end of a particularly tricky bit of knitting and finding herself without yarn enough to finish the task, bustled to a neighbor's house to borrow wool. Her neighbor unceremoniously shut the door in the old woman's face. Sadly for Granny, she was regarded as a busybody, and a suspicious character.

The following morning, what should the door slammer see on her doorstep but a woodchuck. Unfortunately for Granny, later that day a child in that house came down with an illness and died. The untimely death was blamed on Granny Hicks, who it was said had taken on the form of the woodchuck and cast a spell on the household.

That's all it took for Granny to become an official town pariah. Children were allowed to throw stones at her, and one evening five drunk men destroyed her house with axes. Rumor has it that in her rage, Granny, not a little miffed at having just lost her home, pointed a bony finger at each of the young ruffians and foretold the manner of their deaths. Granny Hicks herself died within months, and it is said her predictions regarding the men's deaths all eventually came to pass.

* * *

How often do you get to say, "That witch just plain rocked!"? That's just what Great Island (now known as New Castle Island, off Portsmouth) tavern keepers Alice and George Walton said on a Sunday evening in June 1682. They would continue to utter it for the rest of that coming summer.

The Waltons had settled in for the evening with their family. It was a quiet night, just beginning to darken outside, and they were all gathered in the sitting room. Though it was June, the coming night had brought with it a chill edge. But not cold enough to bring about a hailstorm. . . .

And yet . . . Plink! Plink! Plink! came the sounds of something dinging off the house. George looked up from his reading and traded a quizzical look with his wife. "Hail?"

As soon as he said it, the pelting increased in frequency and soon the roof and exterior walls echoed under the odd attack. The family bolted for the porch and what they saw drew cries of fear and confusion from them.

It had not been hail, but rocks, large and small, raining down on them from the sky, as if they were being attacked by unseen forces hidden in the trees. And then the rocks curved toward them on the porch, as if seeking them out. Several of the projectiles found their marks and elicited cries of surprise and pain from their victims even as the poor people scrambled over one another to get back inside the safety of their home.

Back indoors, Alice assured her husband that no one had been hurt seriously, but George wasn't going to let that keep him trapped inside his own home while someone, or a group of someones, attacked them from without! His rage boiled up inside him, though within moments reason reasserted itself. George bid his family sit in a central room near the fireplace and away from windows, then snatched up the nearest item he could find to defend himself, his axe, just outside the door leading from the kitchen to the woodshed. George paused in the dark—the barrage had lessened. Now would be the ideal time to find who had done this, for surely he would hear them retreating into the safety of the coming gloom of evening and the surrounding woods.

When he cautiously peered outside, the shed door hinges squeaked enough for him to grit his teeth. He pulled up short. He couldn't believe his eyes. It was close to dark, but still light enough for him to see that the dooryard and surrounding yard were littered with rocks, from small pebbles to stones as large as a man's head. He took a dozen steps outside, away from the shed, and a fist-sized stone sailed seemingly out of nowhere and drove into his side. He barked in pain and spun for the door as the sky filled with rocks once again.

He made it back inside, stumbled into the kitchen, and called to his wife. Before she made it to the kitchen, stones whipped through windows, and began zipping through the air in the room, as if looking for targets. It made no sense. Each family member huddled under furniture, covering their heads. George struggled to make it to the middle room where his family hid under furniture, huddled as best they could. Rocks bounced and pounded off walls and table tops, rolled across floors, and even clattered down the chimney, but didn't stop there—they flew across the room. They scattered as from the fire, but nothing caught flame.

The screams of his family were too much to bear—George bellowed for it to stop, knowing of nothing else he could do. Soon the volley slowed, and then all the malevolent noise ceased until the only thing they heard were their own sobs and heavy breathing.

They sat in silence, not daring to move, for long minutes. George was afraid that if he did make any movement at all the bizarre torture might begin again. He was still convinced it was the work of angry neighbors of some sort. But he'd had no clashes with anyone that he knew of, nor had his wife or children—certainly nothing so severe as to warrant such ill treatment.

Eventually they did stir from their spots, and nothing more happened; no rocks flew. His wife lit lamps and began cleaning up the mess, and the children climbed the stairs to their bedchambers. They hadn't been up there more than a minute when they pounded back down the stairs, howling in high dudgeon—something, they shouted, was up there and had chased them downstairs! It had been huffing and snorting and making a terrible, hair-raising racket.

George suspected they were still frightened and wanted to be close to him and his wife. Nonetheless, he checked upstairs and found nothing amiss. He settled the children, and then inspected the rocks in the room. To his surprise, he found a number of them to be hot. And it being June, the fireplace had been kept low, barely a glow for cooking, and supper had been hours before. Nothing would account for the warmed-over stones. With a piece of charcoal, George scribed a mark on a number of the rocks and set them on the table. Turning his back on them to help his wife, he caught her horrified glance and turned to see the rocks he had marked rising from the table of their own accord and flying about the room.

Later, more screams came from his wife and children when they swore they had seen a ghostly hand reaching inward through a smashed window.

It wasn't until the next day that he discovered other oddities—the leading between the smashed windowpane had been bent outward, not inward, indicating whatever had done this had struck them from inside. And he knew that no one in his family had thrown rocks from inside the house. He had only seen rocks whipping at them from unseen hands. That led him to believe this had been the work not of local tricksters but of some supernatural element, some unseen malevolent force from beyond the human realm, beyond the scope of human comprehension.

If the Walton family thought that the previous night's madness was a one-time event, they awoke to find out how very wrong they were. From the start, the hellish torment continued in various ways all day and all night. Walton couldn't go from his house to the barn or to the well or the fields without having to run for cover, for stones would appear as if from nowhere and shower down on him. He took to holding a rough plank over his head whenever he ventured outside.

The unseen enemy soon broadened its repertoire and began hurling anything handy at George, including bricks, chunks of wood, and whatever tools lay at hand. George became cautious about where he laid his ax, sledgehammer, and other tools. This did not prevent the entity from hurling crowbars and mauls at him. The unexpected projectiles launched throughout the

Waltons' property, inside and out, and toward all family members, though mostly toward George Walton, the patriarch, for three months of that summer of 1682.

All of this might seem beyond fantastical, especially if the only historical record of that hellish summer were left by members of the Walton family. But fortunately for the Waltons, a number of non–family members witnessed the strange, inexplicable events. Among them was one Richard Chamberlain, then secretary of New Hampshire colony. He not only saw firsthand the bizarre proceedings, but he went on to write of them, and publish a pamphlet describing them—alas, not until years later.

Understandably, he had been concerned that had he gone public at the time with accounts of what he had witnessed, he might well lose any public credibility he had, not to mention risk his job as a public servant. So he waited sixteen years before publishing his pamphlet, *Lithobolia or the Stone Throwing Devil*, in 1698 in England, which detailed the bizarre episodes he'd witnessed all those years before.

Much speculation has gone into unearthing the cause of the rock throwing. Ghosts or perhaps demons? Angry Indian spirits bent on revenge for the loss of their tribesmembers' lives and lands? Or was it, after all, really just a gang of prank-playing locals? Or had it been, as the local community quickly came to embrace as a cause, the mysterious old woman who lived near the Waltons? The very crone a number of the townsfolk were certain they'd seen up to no-good, secretive, nefarious deeds of late. . . .

And that is who they happily pinned the blame on. Not surprisingly, such behavior only served to stoke the coals that led to the raging inferno of false accusation a mere decade later and just a little to the south—in Salem, Massachusetts.

And that is where the story gains traction in a different direction. In another version, this story is related but is told with a slightly less-than-pitying eye toward our former hero, George Walton. It seems that a widow woman lived in a cabin on a spot of land, and these were the only real things of value she had been left with. Her neighbor, George Walton, had his eye on that land for his own purposes. He tried time and again to buy it from her, but she refused his entreaties. Eventually he resorted to threatening charges of witchcraft, blaming the old girl with various nefarious deeds and difficult-to-disprove (or prove!) accusations. And because such preposterous claims were given credence at the time, the community at large sided with George and against the old widow. She eventually lost her home and land. And who do you think ended up with it? George Walton.

Whether she was a witch or not, it is said that she "laid a ban," or curse, on his newly acquired property, promising Walton that he would never gain from it in profit or pleasure. Walton laughed in her homeless face, ushered her out the door, and ushered his family into the widow's former home.

It is interesting to note that Hannah Jones, the elderly widow accused of witchcraft by George Walton, turned right around and accused Walton of being a warlock. Tit for tat, apparently. It seems they had a long, acrimonious relationship for some time. It also seems that back in 1656, Widow Jones's mother, Jane Walford, had also been accused, tried, and then acquitted of witchcraft. Hmm.

On the one hand that makes her the ideal scapegoat for Walton's ire, as there had been precedent of a sort set in her family, of the sort of behavior that Walton, a known two-faced, contentious Quaker, knew enough to exploit, as it would play on the fears of the local populace. Who in their right minds would want a witch in their midst—and one who might attack at any minute an allegedly innocent family of innkeepers?

By the time Chamberlain had had his fill of staying with the Walton clan and their alleged demonic guest, it was clear he had to summon higher authority. After all, given his reaction sixteen years later in publishing his account for what he believed was a series of "Diabolick Inventions," the authorities would have to be called in. But as luck would have it, once Chamberlain checked out, so did the poltergeist and the witchlike activity. Coincidence? Hardly. Walton probably suspected that once a team of mucky-mucks from the colony government descended, they would discover that he and his family were the instigators of the "Diabolick Inventions."

* * *

And last, but in no way least: In 1656, after Jane Walford of Portsmouth—mother of the accused Hannah (Walford) Jones above—was accused, tried, and acquitted of witchcraft, she wouldn't let the matter lie. She sued her accuser for slander—and won. Score one for the (alleged) witches!

CHAPTER 9

Mountains of Misfortune

The Willey Family's Last Mistake and Other Calamities of the Notches

By the time dawn shone bright on that June morning of 1826, Samuel Willey breathed a sigh of relief as he sipped his coffee. The hellish sounds of the previous night's violent storm still rattled in his head much as they did up and down the vast, steep heart of Crawford Notch. He, his wife, Polly, their five children, and two hired men had lived in this raw, stunning landscape since the previous autumn, and he still hadn't grown accustomed to its savage, fickle ways.

Still, Samuel knew he shouldn't voice much in the way of complaint—it had thus far been a particularly dry spring and they could use the moisture brought by the storm. But he wished, not for the last time that day, that the rain could have come in long, slow doses instead of in such a violent burst.

He parted the curtains and peered out across the river at the awesome sight of Mount Webster's immense bulk. He could glance at it a dozen times a day and still, the same humbling, dizzying feeling overcame him.

Their lives in the Notch were good, and work proceeded at a pace that allowed him to indulge in a slight prideful moment. After all, it hadn't been that long since they had moved in to this abandoned mountainside home. But he had a dream, or rather a vision, his wife jokingly called it. And that was to help make this otherwise forbidding pass more pleasant for people to travel through.

And to her credit, Polly had supported his ambition. They had assumed ownership of the neglected, small home along the rough road through Crawford Notch. He had to admit that the stark power and up-close presence of the mountains—craggy, cold, threatening, and rimmed with clouds or skylined against a sheer, cold blue sky—still had the power to stop him in his tracks daily and pull a long gaze from him.

And that was just what he was doing this morning, his wife by his side, each of them looking out across the valley. And that's when the impossible happened right before them. Samuel was speechless, but his wife was not. Her screams brought their children running.

Before their very eyes the entire mountainside slid soundlessly—for the first few seconds—downward. Then the sound came, a horrible gut-churning grinding din that overrode all reason. It seemed as if the entire mountainside had cut loose and simply slid downslope as if pulled from beneath, as if some cosmic being were playing a joke on them by pulling a rug out from under the mountain. Stunted trees, boulders, scant patches of vegetation, and great washes of gravel all crashed downward in a roaring mass.

For long minutes after the landslides—first a large one, then followed immediately with another, smaller slide—massive boulders continued to dislodge from the craggy heights of Mount Webster, tumbling as if they might keep on rolling, cross the Saco River and the little road before their place, then slam right through their home.

His family's cries brought Samuel Willey out of his awe-struck reverie. He stared at his equally stunned family even as clouds of dust from the still-dry hillside clouded over them. His wife, with trembling hands, clutched as many of her five children as she could to her skirts and returned her husband's shocked stare. She vowed they were leaving right then and there. A profitable winter—though viciously cold and windy it had been—could not make up for what she had just seen.

Part of Samuel wished to agree, but the promise of the place convinced him otherwise. As the hours turned into a day, then two, and the mountainsides about them seemed as infallible as ever, despite the new scars of the landslides, he convinced himself, and finally his reluctant wife, that all would be well, and surely such a freak occurrence could never again happen.

Over the following days and weeks, life began to settle back into a normal routine, as Samuel and his two hired men worked hard to expand the roadside inn to accommodate the increase in traveler and trade traffic that each passing month brought through the Notch.

A few of those travelers eyed the obviously freshly slumped mountainside with suspicion. A good many of them, though tired, opted to continue on through. "That don't look safe to me, mister," said one man, before urging his horses into resuming their journey, albeit at a harder clip, as if the mountain might just decide to repeat its nefarious activities and crush him where he stood.

In the meantime, the more treed, though no less daunting slope behind the house and outbuildings appeared to pose no threat like that they'd witnessed across the narrow valley. But the fact that they still hadn't received any rain since then secretly troubled Samuel. What would that dry weather do to the great blanket of vegetation above and behind them? Would it make it more prone to tearing loose as it had across the river?

One concession he'd made to his wife in his efforts to convince her that staying put was perfectly safe was to build a storm- and landslide-proof shelter just a few hundred feet south of the house. He called it the "camp," but really it was an overturned body of a cart, secured in place. He also wedged a twenty-five-foot log behind the house to help deflect any rocks that might roll down at them.

As the hot, dry summer wore on, they gradually forgot about any far-off dangers of another landslide. There was far too much work to be done just in hauling water, tending the livestock—horses, sheep, pigs, and oxen—repairing and expanding the house and outbuildings, and most important, tending to the travelers.

Still the parching weather persisted, all through June, July, and August.

Then, in the afternoon of a particularly still, cloying Sunday, August 27, 1826, far-off thunderheads—a sight long unseen in those parts—crept closer. It was as if the day were a black cat slowly, carefully, and measurably stalking an unwary field mouse. The bank of roiling dark clouds high up in the forever-blue summer sky rolled slowly toward the Notch.

David Allen, one of the hired men, remarked about it as he and two others stopped for a dipper of water. He sipped, raising the vessel for the last precious drops, and his eyes trailed upward toward the knife-edge ridgeline across the valley. He paused there, squinted sweat from his eyes, and nodded. "Samuel."

His employer looked at him, but the man just nodded toward the sight.

"Well, I'll be," said Willey. And though he knew his first thought should be one of thanks to the Lord for finally providing them with much-needed and precious moisture, there was something sinister to the incoming mass. Each man was thinking back to that terrifying sight of the mountainside slumping before their very eyes following that violent storm back in June. Would it happen again? Surely not, and yet—the conditions were, if anything, even more ripe for a similarly vicious storm.

Willey looked around him and up the long gradual slope behind the house, as if to reassure himself that they were truly safe. He sighed and stretched his back, trying to sound confident. "I certainly hope the Lord sees fit to give us a gentler rain."

The other two men said nothing, but exchanged quick glances of doubt and not a little fear. Willey saw this and leaned close to them. "Please, not a word to Polly or the children that might alarm them."

The others nodded, but a cold clot of dread sat heavily in each of their guts.

By the time early evening came to them, the skies had blackened such that a thick, purple darkness enveloped the Notch house before the clock's usual time for dark to descend. His wife had spoken little, but went about her chores tight-lipped. Samuel knew she was afraid. The children were as well—even the two youngest, Sally and Elbridge, hadn't bickered at the dinner table. By the time his wife had cleared the dishes, a gusting cold wind delivering savage gusts rattled the windows and the first of the big, cold drops of driving rain pummeled the parched homestead. They all bustled in and out, closing windows and battening down whatever lay unattended.

Samuel and the two men buttoned up the barn, locking in the horses, the cow and calf, the sheep, and the chickens. It would soon grow stifling in there as well as in the house, so he made sure to leave enough window space for fresh air to flow.

Finally he and his wife sent the children to bed and they retired to their own room. Samuel sat at the little desk, trying to read from the Bible, as was his custom, but on this night, the Good Book could not engage his interest. The great threatening thunderheads that they had watched all afternoon, building ever closer, began to rumble, slow and bold, uninvited guests, intruders in their midst.

"It's little more than a summer storm, Polly," said Samuel. "It will give us much-needed rain, then pass on elsewhere." He winked at her and then said, "You'll see."

He joined his wife at the front windows, and in the coming gloom, lit bright with slashes of dancing lightning, he realized he was wrong. The Saco River, not far from their home on the other side of the roadway, had already risen and the rain had been falling in earnest but a short while. At that rate, he knew the river would soon flood.

Samuel turned his wife and held her shoulders. "Polly, get the children. I'll get the men. We have to go. I . . . I was wrong. We have to get to the cabin, the shelter, just in case."

Her eyebrows rose suspecting, he knew, what he had left unsaid.

"Don't worry just yet, Polly. But why don't we head to the shelter, just in case."

"But what if the river comes up to it?"

Samuel hadn't thought of that—how foolish he'd been! In all the time he spent building it no one had thought of that eventuality. But looking at the river now, through the lashing rain and brilliant jags of lightning, swelling seemingly with each passing second, he realized escape would be impossible should they secure themselves in the shelter. "We'll just have to run for higher ground."

"But surely we can stay in the house, Samuel." Polly begged him with her eyes.

All he could do was shake his head even as he jumped to action. "Get the children down here, Polly! We have to go. . . ."

The men wasted no time in lighting lanterns and helping to assemble the children, making sure their boots and coats were on, hats pulled down tight.

"Hold hands, everyone. We have to stay together now." Samuel tried to keep his voice steady and a smile on his face, but it was one of the most difficult things he ever had to do. He and his wife each picked up the youngest children and everyone else grabbed tight to one another's belts and coats. "Hold firm now, we're headed straight over that way." Samuel nodded toward twenty-one-year-old hired hand David Nickerson, who was like a son to the Willeys. Nickerson was in the lead, holding aloft a lantern. "Just follow the light and you'll be fine."

Soon they were all outside, shuffling across the yard, glancing downslope toward the rising, roiling fury of the Saco River, which seemed to claw its way closer between each lightning flash. And above, the raw hillside looked as if it might reach out and snatch them. Samuel longed for the night to be over, ached for his family to be safe and sound.

Halfway across the sloped yard, lightning ripped a vast rent in the inky water-filled sky as heavy rain pounded down on them. And in that moment of brilliant, unfortunate clarity, in swinging his head around to shout to make sure his family was accounted for, Samuel Willey saw the most awful thing he ever would see in his entire life. It was also the very last thing he or any member of his family and friends would ever see.

A great raft of living earth moved toward them—it seemed as if the entire mountain had decided to upend itself and drop down on them. Samuel Willey Jr. had time enough for the flicker of a thought to tell him he should scream, but no sound ever came out of his mouth before rocks, gravel, trees, and soil drove into them, pushing, dragging, tumbling, and crushing everyone on the long slope.

The next day, friends from nearby Bartlett came looking for them, following the river to see how their neighbors had fared in the hellish storm. The tempest had swelled the Saco River to many times its normal height, and ripped out homes and barns, crushing them in its mighty, sopping fist. The curious and would-be rescuers found bodies lodged in trees along the route, bloated and ragged carcasses of cows, sheep, horses, goats, and pigs. They found shoes and clothing, and with each step farther into the Notch, their fears grew greater, for the destruction wrought by nature's untamable wrath was plain, stark, and horrifying—and growing worse with each stride forward.

John Barker, a man traveling alone, made his way through the trees, stepping with care over the massive slide of earth stippled with great boulders and the freshly snapped and uprooted trunks and roots of trees. The once-familiar notch was unrecognizable, but he was heartened to see the Willey house, sitting miraculously just where it should be, seemingly unharmed. The attached barn was partially destroyed, but it hadn't affected the house.

Even before he got to the front door, Barker began shouting, hoping for a response from the Willeys. But he received nothing of the sort. The door sat half open, the floor immediately inside a welter of puckering sand and mud—not the sort of thing a visitor to Polly Willey's home would ever encounter, unless something was wrong. Maybe they had made it to safety, but where would they go? Perhaps they had sought safety at Abel Crawford's place. . . .

Barker shouted louder, bursting from room to room. Cowering in a back bedroom he found the family dog, crying and shaking as if gripped with a fever.

Barker managed to coax the beast outside, but the dog bolted downslope and headed in the direction of town.

He thought it curious that little in the house appeared amiss—cups and dinnerware were still on the table, Samuel's beloved family Bible lay open, his reading glasses set beside it. Indeed, the house appeared as if the family had stepped out for a morning of berry picking and would return and pour in through the door any second.

But something told John Barker that he was wrong. Still, he found no sign of the Willey family, or of their hired men, though he did find a few head of their livestock, and wondered if any others were hurt in the damaged barn, but saw none. He continued on to Crawford's place and, bothered that the Willeys weren't there, recruited more neighbors to head in to the Notch to search. He was confident that something was wrong, and hoped that they would not arrive too late with help.

It wasn't until Thursday, August 31, three days after the storm, that a large group of men, some fifty strong, including Samuel Willey's father, brother, and nephews, plus numerous friends and neighbors, finally found the first body. A neighboring farmer named Edward Melcher disturbed a branch and flies clouded the air. He rummaged at the spot in the gravel and discovered a man's hand. Raising the alarm, they soon had the body unearthed.

It was the Willeys' thirty-seven-year-old hired hand, David Allen, a husband and father of four, from nearby Bartlett. But two feet away they found the body of Mrs. Willey. Both of them had been so abused by the landslide that their bodies were stripped naked, their battered faces and bodies barely recognizable.

The searchers knew that soon they might find the others. And just a short time later they found Mr. Willey, his knee jutting from the waters of the Saco, his broken body pinned by a barn timber and twisted in tree roots.

Over the next week, a dwindling number of frantic searchers continued digging. Many reluctantly left off the quest, for they were needed at their own ravaged homes. Days later, near the river, they found the body of the youngest Willey child, Sally, under three feet of sopping gravel. Two hours later, they found

PHOTOGRAPH BY JENNIFER SMITH-MAYO

Fearing they might be crushed in a landslide, in the early morning hours of August 28, 1826, Samuel Willey, his wife, Polly, their five children, and two hired men fled the safety of their home. They were right about the landslide, but they were wrong about leaving the house. They were buried alive in a raft of earth thirty feet thick. The house was untouched.

Eliza Ann, the oldest Willey child. She bore a less-battered appearance than others of her family, and had apparently drowned. But the force of the landslide had also peeled off most of her clothes.

One week after the tragedy, two searchers remained, one of them the young brother of twenty-one-year-old David Nickerson. The young lad told his fellow searcher: "I know my brother is dead, but I must see his body or I shall die." And within days they did find his brother's body, but a few feet from where the first bodies had been found.

Despite further efforts, the last three bodies, those of the children, Jeremiah, Martha, and Elbridge, were never found. Given that the landslide reached thirty feet in depth in places, the searchers had to assume the children were buried deep.

The bodies of those found were buried in a temporary mass grave at the site, then exhumed and reinterred in December. The bodies of the four Willey family members were buried, together, in upper Conway, at a site today known as Intervale. The marker includes the name of all the children. David Allen was buried in Bartlett cemetery, and is marked only by a red granite boulder and a flag, denoting that he had once been a soldier. David Nickerson's grave site is unknown.

The Willey home's near-perfect condition was attributed to the fact that a massive bench of rock just upslope of the structure protected it, diverting the raft of earth as it descended like a massive locomotive down the mountainside. The great tragedy, and the mystery for which we will never have a true answer, is why the family left the safety of their home that fatal night. Obviously Samuel Willey felt he was doing the right thing for his family. Sadly, never has a decision been so wrong.

The storm in the early hours of Monday, August 28, 1826, is still on the record books as having effected the most change to the face of Crawford Notch and much of Saco River Valley itself. It caused tremendous damage up and down the Saco River Valley, and forever altered the landscape.

One family that fared better than the Willeys managed to scramble atop their log cabin as the flood waters rose. What happened next was something they did not expect—as the waters rose, so did their home. Soon they found themselves atop their abode and floating downriver, expecting fully at any moment to be upended and drowned. Instead they rode out the entire dark, stormy night and survived aboard what was left of their floating home—many miles downstream from where they lived.

Years later, once again in August, in the year 1892, the third documented landslide on Mount Mansfield, the highest point in Vermont, stripped a mile-long, half-mile-wide trench down the side of the mountain. At the edge of the massive chasm, a farmer named Oliver Papineau, sure that he was doomed, found in the morning that only his pigpen had been carried away in the night. Fully expecting to find no trace of it, imagine his surprise when a half mile downstream he found not only his pigpen, in relatively decent shape, but also his pig within it, snuffling and rooting in the fresh mud.

* * *

Though there are variations on the following story, they share the same tragic elements: In 1788, a young woman named Nancy had fallen in love with a handsome young farmhand in Jefferson. On the eve of their wedding, in the middle of a brutally cold and snowy winter, young Nancy entrusted to her betrothed her life savings. Alas, it was soon discovered that the young man was more interested in Nancy's cash than in poor Nancy. He absconded with it, and when Nancy got wind of his misdeed, she trailed after him, assuming he had crossed through Crawford Notch in the middle of the night.

It was a thirty-mile hike before her, but Nancy, undaunted and still in love, refused to believe her young man could have done her wrong—and in such a manner. Unbeknownst to her family and friends, she took to the trail in the middle of the night. For hours she trekked deeper into the maw of the largely untraveled mountain wilderness. The howls and blood-stopping screams of hungry, wild mountain beasts surrounded her, and wind whipped frozen, stinging snow in her face.

Half a dozen miles into her journey, Nancy found herself bitterly cold, and exhausted physically and emotionally. She made it to the bank of a half-frozen, rushing stream and with shaking legs and fevered mind, poor Nancy could go no farther. She decided to sit for a few moments to rest, but as soon as she stopped she grew colder and tired, so very tired. She lay down, thinking that she would indulge in a few moments of restorative, delicious sleep.

The next day dawned bright and still and cold. When Nancy's family realized she was nowhere in sight, they expected the worst. And they blamed themselves for not keeping a closer watch on the poor, distraught young woman. They also vowed to track down her deceptive lover and make him pay for his foul deed. But first they must find the distressed girl and soothe her worry.

The more they searched, the greater their fear became. Soon they found a faint trace of tracks leading northward, toward where they suspected her beloved farmhand must have gone—and they feared the worst. Her father and others charged toward the Notch. They trudged for hours, cursing the blowing fresh snow of the previous night, snow that though it amounted to only a few inches, had done its best to obscure the girl's footprints. They found just enough tracks to know she had definitely headed in that dire direction.

Up ridge and down, through deep woods and across fallen boulders. Down again to the small river led the increasingly shorter strides and dragging prints of Nancy—she must have become exhausted. They hoped she had wits enough about her to stop and make a camp; perhaps she had made it to one of the several campsites along the trail that many travelers used on their journeys through the unforgiving White Mountains. Perhaps she had met up with a kindly traveler who had helped her. Though in truth they knew no such person had traveled that way in days.

And then they saw it—the thing they had not wished to see but feared all along—the lump in the snow, no larger it seemed than a child might make. Her father rushed to the spot, crying and hoping and cursing himself and the foul, fickle winter weather. But it was indeed the snow-covered form of his little girl, stone cold and long dead. A sad, lost half-smile on her face, her eyes, once so bright with life and kindness, now grown still and staring at the glittering morning snow through lashes flecked with diamond-like crystals, the cold crystals of death.

Today Mount Nancy, from which Nancy's Brook flows, commemorates the tragic end of that poor girl. But the story does not end there. Indeed, it stretches hundreds of years to modern day. In addition to the local natural landmarks named in Nancy's honor, it is said that anyone today bold enough to hike the same path on a cold, cold autumn evening will hear moans and cries. These mournful sounds rise eerily above the rumble and roar of the frigid mountain freshet. Perhaps they are the cries of the girl, perhaps of her family, perhaps of the farmboy who it is said regretted his actions and went mad with grief over his foul misdeed and his lost love.

And yet, the moans and cries are always followed and overruled by bitter high-pitched laughter. Who could that be?

* * *

In a vicious winter snowstorm early in the nineteenth century, in the frozen heart of Franconia Notch, a well-regarded local teamster by the name of Thomas Boise found himself in the maw of an unexpected storm. His route had become impeded by ever-increasing amounts of snow.

Soon enough, the snow piled up to chest-deep levels. His single horse faltered and could go no farther. Boise knew with all certainty the poor beast would soon expire, so he mercifully killed the horse lest it continue to suffer. But the weather's intensity only increased and within minutes of slaying the horse, Boise knew he, too, would soon lose his struggle with the bone-numbing cold. He had no clothing or coverings of any sort other than the clothes on his back. With trembling hands, he unsheathed his hip knife and painstakingly skinned as much of the still-warm horse as he could.

Inch by inch, he worked the blade against the horse's slowly stiffening flesh, freeing the hide. When he had loosened enough to cover himself, he sliced it free of the carcass and with what felt to him like his last thrust of effort, Boise crawled under a massive nearby boulder. It had lodged there long ago, one edge jutting outward and offering an overhang under which Boise crept, pulling the wet horsehide tightly about himself in hopes that it might at least prevent the killing, chilling wind and driving snow from freezing him as fast than he knew it would.

He was found the following morning by men who had been sent out from the logging camp to search for him. They saw two hooves of the dead horse jutting from a crusted snowdrift. After clearing away the snow, they realized it had been partially skinned. Finding no sign of Boise, they rummaged in the snow all about the carcass. One of the men burrowed over to the rock, half-thinking it might be a logical place for a freezing man to crawl. And he was right.

His shouts drew the other men and they all bent to the task of clearing away the snow to reveal a bizarre snow-and-hair cocoon, stone-stiff to the touch. The men knew because they knocked on it as though it were the front door of a house. "Shhh!" hissed one of the men. "I heard something."

"No you didn't neither, poor Tom's dead. Ain't no man can live—"

"Shut your mouth! I heard him, I tell you!" The big man knelt lower in the snow and nodded, shouting, "We'll have you out of there, Boise Boy, you wait and see!"

With that he nodded at the others, who all set to digging at the snow. One of the men shucked his bullhide chopper mittens and scratched and clawed where the hide met the snow. He began to widen a gap enough to sneak his fingertips underneath the stiff edge and pry upward on the stiff, raw hide. But it was not enough. "The axes, men! But be careful!"

Two of the more skilled axmen set to working the hide gently but with firmness and split the frozen hide enough for the others to pry it apart to reveal their friend, Thomas Boise, huddled like a baby with his knees drawn tight to his chest and his hands wedged deep within his coat.

"Make a fire! Make a fire!" shouted the big man, at no one and everyone all at once, even as he gingerly scooped up his wiry friend in his arms and slid him slowly outward.

He knew Boise was alive because one of his eyes miraculously fluttered as though it were a moth's wing. A faint trickling cloud of breath leaked out one nostril. He tried to open his mouth but only succeeded in eliciting a wheezing cry. But Thomas Boise lived to tell of his raw adventure.

Today the glacial erratic under which he huddled, wearing the raw skin of his dead horse, is marked with a plaque and can be viewed—and even laid under—just off Route 93, Franconia Notch. Reenactment of Boise's adventure is not recommended in winter.

CHAPTER 10

Cryptic Creatures

Devil Monkeys, Thunderbirds, and Bigfeet . . . Oh My!

Cryptozoology is the search for and study of creatures whose very existence hasn't yet been proven, the most common of which are the Loch Ness monster and Sasquatch. But just because definitive proof hasn't yet been officially located doesn't mean these beasties aren't roving the depths or prowling the forests—even in New England. In fact, some of them are closer than Yankees might think. Just ask the hundreds of eyewitnesses through the centuries. As with much in the history of New England, one needn't leave the region to find ample and convincing accounts that strange creatures, the likes of which most of us may never see, populate this complex, mountainous region.

There have been numerous sightings in New England throughout the nineteenth and twentieth centuries of large, well-muscled, hair-covered humanoids who move with astonishing

speed, exude pungent odors, and who were both seen and reciprocated with curious stares. As with many such sightings, in New
England, they might begin in one small state but frequently end
up in another. It seems borders don't much impress Bigfeet.

For nearly a century, beginning in August 1895 and occurring
well into the 1970s, the town of Winsted, Connecticut, was home
to a number of reported sightings of a hairy fellow who came to be
called the Winsted Wild Man. Far northern Vermont was said to
have been terrorized for many years in the late eighteenth and early
nineteenth centuries by a mean-spirited creature described as an
upright, naked bear known as "Old Slipperyskin." Could it have
been a Sasquatch with mange or just an oversize nudist?

The state of Maine has a long history of sightings and close
encounters with Sasquatch-like creatures, particularly in the wilderness region surrounding Mount Katahdin. As recently as 1988,
a troop of Boy Scouts watched a massive, hairy man-creature
upslope from them, ripping up roots, presumably searching for
food. They noted it had long, reddish hair, a wedge-shaped face,
and that it stunk to high heaven of rotten eggs.

The Nutmeg State is no stranger to Sasquatch sightings. In
1992 a Connecticut dairy farmer encountered a massive man-
beast in his barn early one morning. The creature, eight feet
tall and covered in shaggy hair, was apparently as startled as the
farmer and fled within seconds.

Numerous sightings, some as recent as the past couple of
years, continue to occur throughout New England, notably in

New Hampshire and New England history abound with stories of encounters with Bigfoot and other rarely seen beasties. Founded by renowned author and cryptozoologist Loren Coleman, the International Cryptozoology Museum in Portland, Maine, is a great place to learn about odd creatures of all shapes and sizes. In fact, the above image of Bigfoot was captured there. . . .

Massachusetts's Hockomock Swamp, in the dark heart of what is often referred to as Bridgewater Triangle. This anomaly-filled region, in which all manner of strangeness is recorded, is much the same as New Hampshire's Ossipee Triangle.

And speaking of New Hampshire, plenty of beastly encounters have taken place in the Granite State—enough to raise eyebrows and quicken the pulses of even the most stalwart citizen. Take Coos County, for instance. As one would expect, given the fact that it is both heavily forested and sparsely populated, this northernmost county in the state has seen its share of Sasquatch activity. One of the most recent encounters occurred during hunting season, in mid-November 2004. Before sunup, two men hiked into a remote area familiar to them, confident that day would find them bagging a buck fit for the record books.

Unfortunately for them, something else had other plans. As the sun rose, a high-pitched screaming and squealing erupted a hundred yards from them, up a game trail. They looked toward the hair-raising sounds and in the growing morning light they saw the unmistakable figure of a dark, hair-covered man, approximately seven feet tall, and with a somewhat pointy head. The two astounded hunters watched as the creature continued its howling and then eventually departed. They also fled, but returned a short time later, having built up enough nerve to venture to the spot where the creature had been. It left humanlike footprints that measured fifteen to eighteen inches long, and with a stride of up to six feet—far too long to have been those of a human. The frightened men did not hunt that property for the rest of that year, but have since returned in hopes of seeing another such creature.

And then there's the singular 1987 experience of Walter Bowers Sr. While out hunting birds in late September, near Mill Brook, in Salisbury, New Hampshire, he sensed somehow that he was not alone, and grew concerned that someone else might be hunting nearby. As a lifelong sportsman, Bowers knew that an oversight in the field could quickly result in tragedy. Meanwhile, the feeling that this other someone was actually watching him became more profound. And that's when he saw it: A massive manlike creature, roughly nine feet tall, covered with gray hair, and with hands similar in shape to a man's . . . but three times larger.

The two individuals, hunter and man-beast, stared at each other for a few long seconds, then Bowers took off, with backward glances assuring him that the massive creature was doing the same—in the opposite direction.

Bowers ended up telling the local police, though he got the sense they were only humoring him in listening to his tale. He then related the incident to the game warden, who did laugh, and intimated that what the experienced hunter had no doubt seen was a bear, or perhaps a moose.

Eventually a newspaper reporter took the story seriously and trekked back to the spot with the armed man. They found nothing, but the reporter told his readers that he believed Mr. Bowers, positing the notion that Bowers didn't strike him as the sort of man who would open himself up to public ridicule, which a story such as his would surely earn him.

In New Hampshire's Squam Mountain region in the central part of the state, a man was driving with his family at night when a massive hairy man with a triangular-shaped face bounded into the road, stared at the car's headlights for a few moments, and then dashed back into the woods.

Carroll County, located in the east-central region of the state, has experienced more Bigfoot sightings than any other New Hampshire county. In the 1930s, in the Chocorua Valley, an eight-foot-tall manlike creature, walking upright and covered in black hair, was seen a number of times stealing chickens at several local farms. The curious thing about it—other than the fact that it was a Bigfoot—is that all those who witnessed it said it smelled so foul they referred to it as a skunk bear. They were also quick to point out that this was definitely not a bear.

In May, 2002, a vacationing family drove northward from Boston to Conway, the night fully dark in the hill country at nine p.m. In no great hurry, the father stopped along the side of the road and instructed his son to shine into the roadside trees the spotlight they used for viewing wildlife. Soon they spotted glowing red eyes, and then a massive, upright creature covered in dark hair emerged from the gloom. It stood on the far side of a cable guardrail, watching them, one hand resting atop as if it were about to jump over. The startled father described the beast as looking like a three hundred-pound gorilla with a head like an upright watermelon. He also had seen enough bears in his life that he knew this was no black bear.

In Rockingham County, in August 2003, while walking in the woods, two friends heard the distinctive sounds of a creature approaching. They stopped and stood still, hoping they might see a deer or some other wild animal. But it wasn't a deer that emerged from the thick forest. Not far away, a tall creature covered in long, coarse black hair walked by . . . and didn't once look at them. They later described it as most definitely a manlike creature, but with unusually long, droopy arms. And it walked by on two legs.

On May 7, 1977, near the grounds of a Hollis, New Hampshire, flea market, Gerald St. Louis and two preteen boys had camped so as to stake out a prime spot the next morning to sell their goods. After dark, St. Louis exited his van, backlit by the interior light, and came face-to-face with an eight- or nine-foot-tall hair-covered man. The startled Bigfoot bolted toward a four-and-a-half-foot-high fence, and leapt it with ease. The flea market hopefuls hopped in the van and blazed on out of there, not bothering to gather up their sellable goods.

A little while later, and a few hundred yards away, two other flea marketers sat in their truck, also hoping for an early start and good digs at the coming morning's sale. But when their truck began shaking, and they looked to see if they were in the midst of an earthquake, they, too, spied a massive hairy creature. It took off and so did they.

Both St. Louis and the other two men all ended up back at the flea market the following day, where they met and were able to corroborate each other's stories. They worked up enough nerve to inspect the region for evidence of the creature, and found seventeen-inch-long footprints, but nothing else . . . other than their memories and a shared steadfast refusal to believe they'd seen anything other than a New Hampshire Bigfoot.

* * *

The Thunderbird is one of the oldest myths of unknown creatures in New England. Though often more associated with tribes of Plains Indians, it was also firmly rooted in the folk tales of the Algonquin Indians of the Northeast, and was regularly seen by the various tribes of the region. It has been described as a frightening, winged man-shaped creature with a smallish head and a body larger than an average man's. In place of arms, the thing sported great leathery wings twice as long as it was tall. Tales say that though it didn't seem interested in devouring humans, it would on occasion do so. When in attack mode, it resembled a huge raptor, folding into a killing dive and emitting a frightening screech as it dove at great speeds.

Unfortunately—or not—the creature was last seen in the northeast in Pennacook, New Hampshire, at the beginning of the sixteenth century. Or was it? Consider the curious case of Devil's Den, a gaping black hole on Mount Willard, in Crawford Notch, reputed to be the very grisly home of ol' Scratch, aka the Devil, himself. Or rather one of his demon spawn (perhaps a version of the Thunderbird?). None other than Abel Crawford—namesake of that very notch—is said to have explored this cave in 1800. But it is an account of a subsequent visit, sometime prior to 1850, that makes reference to a gruesome discovery: The floor of the cave was strewn with the skeletal parts and pieces of an untold number of creatures, both wild and human.

A number of anecdotal accounts over the years state that it was the lair of none other than a massive, leather-winged creature that departed the safety of its lair at dusk and went hunting to feed on the flesh of beasts and men. Perhaps this really was the lair of the Thunderbird? (Never mind that the cave has been bereft of bones since at least 1858, when Dr. Benjamin Ball was lowered to the entrance on ropes. Expecting to find bears, he had armed himself with a knife, but was somewhat disappointed to find little more than dust and a few feathers.)

Motorists heading north along Route 302 in Crawford Notch can catch a glimpse of the gaping dark hole, high up on Mount Willard's craggy face. And if they look long enough, they might well see something moving just inside the shadows.

Did it die away when the people who most believed in it intermingled with whites? Apparently not, because in 1971, a massive birdlike creature with a twelve-foot wingspan was seen at Taunton Bird Hill in Massachusetts. Two decades later, in 1992, it was again seen at the same place, and was described as manlike, but with wings. Given that New England is a relatively small region, it is no surprise, then, that a few years ago a similar creature was spotted at night along a rural stretch of Route 55 near New Milford, Connecticut. The two people traveling westward in their automobile both witnessed a massive bird with a ten-foot wingspan that they each described as reminding them of a pterodactyl.

Though the mysterious manlike raptor beast was last seen winging over New Hampshire's mountainous landscape hundreds of years ago, it has been seen not too far to the south, and much more recently. Perhaps it tired of waiting for summer tourists and their little dogs, and decided to head south in hopes of finding tastier pickings.

* * *

Unlike many human encounters with inexplicable creatures, those of cryptozoological origin, the New Hampshire residents' encounters with the "Devil Monkey" have taken place in recent memory. The tiny town of Danville, New Hampshire, located in the southeast corner of the state, is decidedly not the sort of place one would expect to catch sight of . . . a Devil Monkey! But that is just what happened on a night in early September 2001, when the town's fire chief, David Kimball, became one of a dozen people to witness the freakish beast when it bounded into the street, appearing confused and agitated. Before anyone could move, it dashed off out of sight again.

For the most part, the group stood for long seconds in stunned silence. Surely they couldn't have seen what they did just see? But they conferred and their facts matched up: It had been a large hairy creature reminiscent of a primate, but with a whole lot of dark brown hair, reddish-tinged, and with long claws and a long tail. Some witnesses saw sharp-looking pointed teeth in a long snout such as one would expect to find on a dog, along with pointed ears that jutted from the sides of its head, close to the top. They also agreed that it measured roughly eight feet long from nose to tail tip.

It was heard by a number of people in town throughout that day making a hooting, howling, hollering sound.

Today the creature those dozen Danvillians witnessed is thought to have been an escaped zoo animal, or perhaps a pet someone set free once it grew out of its cute baby monkey phase. Several groups of residents set out to track and capture the creature, but turned up empty-handed.

The Danville sighting interested cryptozoologists because it was not the first—but it was the first time a "Devil Monkey" was seen this far north. Since the early 1920s, such creatures have been sighted a number of times in the southern Appalachian mountain chain. It has been blamed for a number of savaged household pets, wild animals, and even small livestock. Since the Green and White Mountains form the northern end of the Appalachian chain, it is conceivable that these primate-like beasts are expanding their range as the climate continues to change.

* * *

Native cultures all over the world share remarkably similar stories about a number of creatures said to be mischievous and ultimately harmful toward humans. These creatures are known in Scandinavian countries as trolls and dwarfs, by the Cornish as bucca, by the Irish as leprechauns, by the British as gremlins, by Americans as tommyknockers, and by certain Native American tribes as, among other names, the pukwudgies. In recent times, many such little men have come to be regarded and represented in popular culture as little more than mischievous creatures. While in cautionary tales they perform harmless trickery, or lead a human to unexpected treasure, their real-life victims often report them to be demonic, sadistic, and brutal.

The Vale End Cemetery in Wilton, New Hampshire, is said to be one of the most haunted in New England. Much of it is owed to the alleged existence of demonic little creatures and the vast number of people who have witnessed them. The diminutive devils have been described as roughly two feet tall, with hairy bodies, pot bellies, and large noses. They don't appear particularly harmful, but they are said to exude an aura that unnerves those who witness them.

New England is no stranger to sightings of little people. Long before white Europeans came to these shores, small manlike creatures were believed to exist by each of a number of native tribes of the northeast region. From Canada's Cree we have the Mennegishi, tiny men with oversize noseless heads and large eyes.

Maine's Penobscot Indians call their wee folk Wanagemeswak, while another Maine-based tribe, the Passamaquoddy, claim two distinct types of tiny people, the Nagumwasuck and the Mekumwasuck, both roughly three feet tall and rather unbecoming to behold.

Given the similarity in descriptions of all these little people, it is interesting to note that the most famous—and quite recent—sightings of just such a creature happened on April 21–22, 1977, to four different teenagers in Dover, Massachusetts, in a single night. Dubbed the "Dover Demon" by world-renowned author and cryptozoologist Loren Coleman, the creature was reported as being small, pink-/peach-colored, large-headed, and with long, slender limbs and tendril-like fingers. The youths' testimonies corroborated one another, and no evidence turned up of chicanery or collusion.

Sometimes New England's little people appear in groups. A population of wee folk was said to reside, well into the twentieth century, on an island in the middle of the 410-mile Connecticut River, somewhere near Springfield, Massachusetts. They were seen for three years, watched from shore with binoculars, spotted by airplane—and then appeared no more.

Long ago, there purportedly existed a race of little folk on an island in Beaver Lake in Derry, New Hampshire. They were believed to exist for a long time by local Indians and later, by the Scots-Irish who settled the region.

More recently a man in Derry, New Hampshire, while engaged in chopping down Christmas trees on December 15, 1956, happened to look up—perhaps he felt he was being watched. The image of what he saw stayed with him for years: A two-foot-tall elephant-hided creature, but with green skin, stood staring at him from several feet away. It had a large head with a big forehead area, similar to other such creatures sighted in New

England. Its ears were more like a dog's ear flaps, and in place of its nose, it had two small holes, above which sat large, filmy eyes.

In place of long, slender fingers, however, this creature is said to have arms and legs with stumplike endings. The tree cutter and the wee green man regarded each other for twenty minutes, at which point the intrepid tree cutter lunged at the little man in an attempt to capture it. The wee creature screeched such that the tree cutter fled, abandoning not only his entrepreneurial pursuit of creature-napping, but also his Christmas trees and ax.

* * *

And last, but certainly not least, we come to the Wolfman of Clark's Trading Post, denizen of a ramshackle, junk-strewn cave in the Lincoln region, deep in the heart of the Whites of New Hampshire. The dreaded Wolfman is one of the most frequently sighted of all inexplicable creatures, and has, over the past several decades, frightened thousands of children and their parents. He appears to be a somewhat accomplished rough beast, and has been witnessed by many, roaring by in his smoke-spewing jalopy, clad in skins, covered in hair (hard to tell where the furs end and his own pelt begins), eye patch covering one peeper, firing off a shotgun, and howling at those he claims are trespassing on his property.

Part wolf, part man? Who knows? But he doesn't show sign of going away anytime soon. A summertime visit to Clark's Trading Post, in Lincoln, preferably with the entire family, is a near-certain way to catch sight of this wild, hairy rogue. But be forewarned: He's as irascible, unsavory, and mysterious as they come.

CHAPTER 11

The Lost Madonna

...and Other Valuables Vanished in the White Mountains

Just how did a solid silver statue of the Madonna come to be lost in the White Mountains of northern New Hampshire? It all began in 1759, during the famous French and Indian War. The war, which lasted from 1754 to 1763, began as a series of small skirmishes between the British and the French Canadians.

By the time 1759 rolled around, the French, with bands of Abenaki Indians as their allies, had been raiding the various border settlements established by British colonists along the Canadian border with New England and New York. They felt sure that this guerrilla-type warfare was most effective in discouraging further unwanted settlement. But they hadn't reckoned on stirring into action one Lord Jeffrey Amherst, commander at the time of both Fort Ticonderoga and Crown Point. Amherst summoned British Army Major Robert Rogers, leader of the now-famous Rogers' Rangers, a band of tough-as-nails guerrilla fighters known for sometimes brutal, but effective tactics.

Repeated bloody cross-border raids by the Indians against white British settlers usually resulted in the kidnapping of men, women, and children. Following these incursions, Indian raiders force-marched their captives north, and then ransomed them back to their families. Lord Jeffrey Amherst decided that enough was enough. He summoned Rogers and his hardy band of fighting men, and a raid on the Indian village of St. Francis was mapped out.

The village itself had been established by Jesuits who had been trying, with slow, mixed results for a century, to convert the Abenaki to Christianity. They had had better results with the Huron, and so were able to establish a modest Catholic mission north of the border in Quebec, just above Lake Memphremagog. They named their new spiritual center St. Francis.

But the Abenaki, it seemed, couldn't let their anger at the English settlers abate. And their raiding parties into the still-wild frontier region of northern New England were often profitable— and exciting—affairs. It was believed by the largely Protestant English that the Jesuits were responsible for inciting and perpetuating this bloodlust against the English, and so a raid on St. Francis was arranged.

Rogers gathered his able and loyal troops and planned what they intended to be a hard-hitting and hopefully decisive raid on St. Francis, just over the border in Quebec. If all went according

Robert Rogers.
Commandeur der Americaner.

In the fall of 1759, Robert Rogers led his band of fighters, Rogers'
Rangers, northward to St. Francis, Quebec, on a raiding mission
they hoped would prevent future cross-border attacks by the Abenaki.
Heavy-handed tactics resulted in many deaths and the theft of the
village chapel's relics. But on their return trip south, the scattered
Rangers nearly starved—and resorted to cannibalism to remain alive.

to plan, the village—notorious as a known staging area for similar raids against the colonies—would be taken by surprise.

On September 13, Lord Amherst sent Rogers his orders for the raid. Among his directives: "Remember the barbarities that have been committed by the enemy's Indian scoundrels on every occasion, where they had an opportunity of showing their infamous cruelties on the King's subjects, which they have done without mercy. Take your revenge, but don't forget . . . it is my orders that no women or children are killed or hurt."

Unfortunately, the last directive would be ignored.

On September 13, 1759, Major Rogers and 220 men departed, traveling only in dark lest the large contingent be spied from shore. They left Crown Point in a long, silent line of boats, each man equipped with an oar and, bending their backs to the task, they glided up Lake Champlain. The three-week trek northward to St. Francis was fraught with hardship, accidents, and illness, resulting in many men turning back. Still Rogers pressed on.

On September 23, the Rangers, now numbering 140, slid into shore at Missisquoi Bay, the farthest point they were able to go with their seventeen whale boats. Rogers left the boats and vital supplies—primarily food—crucial to a successful return trip, with two trusted Indians guarding them. Unbeknownst to Rogers, his large contingent of men had been followed for some time, due to increased patrols of French soldiers in the area, likely because of the recent British victory at Quebec.

Once Rogers and his men took to shore and struck out for St. Francis, French patrols seized the whale boats and supplies. They kept a number of them, and destroyed the rest. The loss of his boats and supplies would prove a crippling blow to Rogers's expedition on his return trip. The discovery of the boats also tipped off the French to the sizable British presence. The French guessed correctly that Rogers's men were headed for St. Francis and sent word to the surrounding French and Indian forces to prepare for a retaliatory attack.

It took Rogers's men a week of hard work just to make it through a boggy, swampy landscape. The pursuing French patrols became overwhelmed by the harsh conditions and gave up the chase. By October 3, Rogers's men made it to within a few miles of their targeted village, though now they were upstream and across the river from St. Francis. They worked fast to chop down trees to make rafts to ferry themselves and their gear across the St. Francis River, a fast-moving flow.

Ironically, most of the Abenaki men of the village were out patrolling with the French, looking for the British forces that had the week before abandoned their boats at Missisquoi Bay. St. Francis was a bustling place that night of October 3. Rogers bedecked himself in Indian garb and crept into the village, hoping to glean any scrap of information that might help them in their attack. He learned the Abenaki were engaged in a celebration of sorts, a war dance, perhaps to search for himself and his men. Unfortunately for Rogers, another member of his party, a Mahican Indian, slipped into the village and warned them of the impending attack. This reduced the number of civilians left in the village. Despite this, in the early morning hours that followed, Rogers and his men crept close to the village, split up into a number of smaller groups, and by five a.m., they were ready to launch their attack.

Rogers led his men in their no-holds-barred attack. House doors were kicked in, startling residents sleeping off the excesses of the previous night's festivities. Before they could rise, Rogers and his men cut them low, stabbing and clubbing and tomahawking them in their beds. Those villagers—women, men, children, the elderly, it didn't matter—who fled the violence-filled town were soon dropped in their tracks by yet more armed rangers outside of town. Others who no doubt felt as though they might make it away in safety had reached their canoes. They launched them and paddled frantically, only to be caught. The canoes, along with the Abenaki inside—including children—were sunk and their passengers drowned.

Soon the raid was a decided victory. Rogers gave orders to burn the village. Yet more screams were heard when villagers who had hidden themselves in their homes were burned alive. The church, too, was looted, then razed.

The band of rangers ransacked the small Catholic chapel, and while several men stood watch in the doorway, and others stayed outside, weapons drawn, the men inside the chapel ran riot, snatching anything they felt they could carry and that looked to be of potential worth. A gold chalice atop the altar made its way into a cloth sack, as did a large, heavy pair of gold candlesticks, a cross, and other small silver items. Wine and other comestibles were sought, but the men were disappointed in those meager findings. But the prize that captivated them, giving them pause for a moment, was a demure, but solid-silver statue of the Virgin Mary.

"Men! Make haste!"

It was Major Rogers himself, barking orders. The men in the chapel grumbled, felt cheated of their rightful loot, but knew, too, that their leader was correct—the time to flee was upon them. They were straggling and knew that the main contingent of their force would not wait for them. They also knew that their enemy, the French and Indians, would soon find the village a slaughterous ruin and gather their forces. It would not do to be caught straggling.

Rogers had kept a few villagers hostage and interrogated them, thus learning that they would soon be outnumbered by roughly four hundred French and Indian fighters due to arrive in St. Francis the following day. Knowing they would never make it back to their boats—and suspecting that their boats and supplies had been found—Rogers determined that their best means of escape lay in a two hundred-mile trek south through raw, unmapped wilderness.

Major Rogers's men were ill equipped, exhausted, and strung out in too long a line to prove effective in a fight. Their only sustenance lay in what meager rations of corn they managed to carry away from the village with them. As the French and Indians closed in, brimming with renewed hate toward the British, they picked off Rogers's numerous stragglers, their bodies looted for whatever might be of use to the French and Indian fighters, who then moved on, bloodlust giving them extra incentive to push ahead, to catch up with the rest lest they get too far into their own familiar land.

In an effort to confuse the enemy and to save as many of his men as he could, Rogers ordered his rangers to split into smaller bands. But their pursuers did the same and the men being sought realized their flight and desired escape was beginning to become less of a certainty and more of a hope.

Soon enough, that hope dissolved into a slurry of blood as four men who were carrying some of the looted holy relics were nearly overcome by blood-stirred Indians and French soldiers by the shores of the mighty Connecticut River. The men persisted in carrying their ill-gotten goods as one of the four, knowing the region and also knowing how very close their pursuers were, begged the other three to follow him. He led them into the mountains, between towering crags known as the Great Notch.

Gaunt from lack of sleep and food, and having barely slaked their dire thirst only enough to keep themselves moving forward, the weary rangers climbed higher until they reached a jutting shelf of gray-black granite in the rocky terrain.

Far below them roiled the Israel River, swollen with autumn rains. "Well, this is grand! Just what do we do now?" gulped a thin, rat-faced man once his breathing had slowed.

"Keep your voice down," said another man in a hoarse whisper, glowering at the fool and listening, as were the other two, for the certain sound of their newly alerted pursuers. Sure enough, he heard overlapping, hurried voices, indicating they had heard the fool ranger's outburst.

"We must fly from here," growled the man familiar with the region. Without hesitation he snatched the sack containing the silver statue of the Madonna from the reedy man and hurled it outward.

"No!" shouted the fool, his begrimed arms outstretched toward his dropping prize, his hands grasping, clawlike, at nothing.

For a brief moment, all four men watched the sack flutter as it dropped, then separate itself from the silver statue and drift behind, falling slower—much slower than the silver lady, which entered the roiling brown waters far below with a gulping splash that seemed to them all a far less worthy treatment than the Holy Mother deserved.

"What have you done?" said the rat-faced man. "Do you not know how much that was worth?"

"More than our lives?" growled one of the other men, already following the other two along the edge of the cliff.

The fool had no more time for brooding, because he heard voices close by. And they were not voices he wanted to hear—they were foreign voices, angry voices, the voices of the enemy, French and Indian fighters. He scrambled to catch up with his group farther along the cliff face.

But their flight was short-lived. A handful of fighters had positioned themselves further along the top of the cliff, just above and out of sight of the hunted men, and at a sign from their fellows, they waited until the four fatigued but still skittish rangers emerged. One by one, they slew the rangers and hurled their bodies from on high, dropping them down into the same rushing waters into which those four men had but minutes before watched their beloved prize, the silver statue of Mother Mary, disappear.

Many years later, hunters eventually found the remains of these men, pursuing and retracing their path of flight, having pieced together as many of the details of the missing looted prizes as they could.

More brutal than the slaughter at St. Francis are the stories of the degraded state in which the remnants of Rogers's forces found themselves during their flight. The disparate—and desperate—bands of rangers had to resort to cannibalism before they reached safety. Several English fighters, caught by the French, were found to be carrying human flesh. Their throats were slit. Despite the apparent dismal outcome, Rogers and his men were treated as heroes. The village of St. Francis was rebuilt.

Over sixty years later, in 1816, other curious treasure seekers found the golden candlesticks along the shores of Lake Memphremagog, an international water that stretches from Quebec southward into Vermont. But to date, no one has ever located the gold chalice, the cross, or the large silver statue of the Virgin Mary. She is believed to still be hidden somewhere in or near the Israel River, near Jefferson, New Hampshire, patiently waiting for someone to discover her and take her home. Her worth in silver is said to be in the hundreds of thousands of dollars. But her intrinsic historic value is priceless.

* * *

It was the early successes of the burgeoning American Revolution that began in 1763 that first roused a number of well-fed and underworked British bureaucrats to scratch their chins and shift their bellies. They began to consider the remote possibility that the pesky rebels might just gain the upper hand in what they had hoped would be a minor kerfuffle. And one of the bureaucrats who had more reason than many others to fear for his and his wife's welfare and future in the colonies was New Hampshire Governor John Wentworth, in office from 1767 to 1775.

A devout Loyalist, Wentworth was born in Portsmouth, New Hampshire, in 1737. He was named after his grandfather, John Wentworth, lieutenant governor of the province of New Hampshire in the 1720s, and his uncle was Governor Benning Wentworth. John the second earned his bachelor's and master's degrees from Harvard College, and while there was chummy with future president John Adams.

To be fair, Wentworth, though a wealthy landowner, was not unsympathetic to the woes inflicted on the common colonist under British rule. He even had a hand in influencing the eventual repeal of the hated Stamp Act.

In 1749 his uncle, Governor Benning Wentworth, added to his own fortunes by selling land grants west of the Connecticut River. Unfortunately for him, this was land he had no right to sell. The governor's greed caused major headaches. This land was eventually awarded to the province of New York, though the people who lived there, among them Ethan Allen and his Green Mountain Boys, disputed these efforts. The territory they occupied eventually became the state of Vermont. But poor bumbling Governor Benning Wentworth was caught with his pudgy pink fist in the cookie jar. Rather than seeing him run off in disgrace, young John Wentworth, later known as Sir John Wentworth, First Baronet, persuaded the powers that be to let his disgraced uncle retire with his tatty dignity still somewhat intact, and replace him with young John.

And so in 1766, John was commissioned governor and vice admiral of New Hampshire, as well as surveyor general of the woods in North America. During his tenure as governor, the state was divided into five counties and he named them after British leaders of the time, as well as some of his own relations. He was also responsible for the first large-scale construction of roads linking large towns, thus enabling and increasing trade, and during his tenure as governor, his surveyor produced what is considered the first detailed map of the region.

Militarily, he beefed up the province's militia from 10,000 poorly disciplined, ill-equipped troops to 11,600 and three regiments. Though he was largely popular with colonists of his province, Wentworth began to slip in the ratings as unrest increased in Massachusetts. The Battles of Lexington and Concord, on April 19, 1775, proved a dire turning point for him.

From then on, Wentworth's life grew more complicated until, on June 13, 1775, an armed mob surrounded his Portsmouth mansion and aimed a cannon at the front door. Wentworth and his family were able to flee, and made their way to the relative safety of Fort William and Mary, on the island of New Castle, just off Portsmouth. He eventually traveled by sea to Boston, and then sent his family to England. He remained in Boston until 1776, when New York City fell to the rebels. He sailed for England early in the new year of 1778 and eventually moved to Halifax, where from 1792 to 1808 he held the post of lieutenant governor, the first civilian governor of Nova Scotia.

What does all this have to do with treasure in the White Mountains? Quite a bit, as it turns out. You see, when Wentworth and his family fled, under direct threat of cannon fire, from his Portsmouth mansion, it is reported he did so with seven hastily stuffed trunks brimming with all manner of valuable personal property. He ferried this load northward, toward his other mansion, in Wolfeboro, along the Old Dover Road, with all haste.

But the unforgiving terrain did not agree with his plans. Soon Wentworth was forced to accede that the heaviness of the cargo was slowing what should have been a flight for their lives. He couldn't risk the possibility of being caught as the colonists' blood was up, and as an officer for the Crown, he was a prime target for the revolutionaries' ire.

Wentworth's team plodded slower and slower when, with a disgusted growl at the situation in which he found himself, Wentworth halted the overloaded wagon. It was plain to him that this situation had become untenable. Despite his wife's pleas to the contrary, he began unloading the seven chests, intending to come back for them when what he hoped would be a short-lived revolution had died down. Surely the colonists could not sustain what, he had to admit, had been revealed as a spirited and not altogether unplanned series of attacks on British holdings and forces.

For the moment, we will leave his trunks of riches, safely hidden, allegedly one of them brimming with coins carrying a value at the time of $25,000, the remaining half-dozen trunks hastily crammed with all manner of silver goods.

We will instead direct our attention to a slightly different version of that story, one in which we still find Governor Wentworth in rapid flight from the bloodthirsty hordes of freedom fighters. In this one, he was nearly trapped at his Smith's Pond mansion, but managed to gain the road toward Portsmouth and the relative safety of the British fleet docked there. He was, naturally, accompanied by his wife and, sadly for him, a brace of horses that were losing strength by the second, their load was that great. Wentworth resigned himself to the fact that lightening the load was the only solution should they hope to stand a chance of reaching safety at Portsmouth.

Despite his wife's protestations—which made her, however briefly in his frustrated, tired eyes, a candidate for also being left behind—he unloaded a single chest filled to capacity with much of their personal fortune in the form of cold, hard coin-based cash and silver plates, candlesticks, silverware, and more. With a stern look, presumably as a warning to his fair lady to keep her mouth shut, Wentworth dragged the laden chest to a secret spot off the road and buried it, intending to return for it as soon as this unpleasant episode had passed. The governor and his wife resumed their journey, pulled along by still tired but no doubt somewhat relieved horses.

As with the previous version of the story, Wentworth, for reasons of personal safety, never found the time or ability to return for his abandoned loot. And so its location continues to remain an intriguing mystery, somewhere in the wilds—or perhaps not so wilds—of New Hampshire today, with many amateur treasure hunters agreeing that it remains unfound somewhere in the region of Durham.

* * *

During the French and Indian War, Abenaki and other tribes regularly dropped down below the Canadian border and raided British colonists' settlements, causing no end of mayhem, terrifying settlers, and leaving behind a trail of smoking ruin, murder, and terrorized survivors. Those who weren't killed, though, were usually herded into long lines and force-marched, ill-treated, north into Canada, where they would be used as trade goods, living tools of extortion. In time, they were ransomed back to their villages and families.

Often paid in gold and silver, but also in jewelry, silverware, and baubles, the going rate the English paid for their loved ones ranged from five pounds sterling for children up to more than fifty pounds sterling for adult males.

No matter what the Indians were paid in, it seemed they were more interested in the game than the prize. Fueled by a century of resentment and revenge against the British colonists for usurping their homelands, the tribes' fires of anger were stoked by the French, who supplied the Algonquin and other tribes with arms and ammunition.

Ironically, the Indians had little use for the gold, silver, and other so-called valuables the English eagerly traded for the release of their loved ones. But the Indians were savvy enough to know that draining the English colonists of these goods would eventually weaken the English. And so the Indian raiders regularly hauled great loads of blood money and goods, depositing the laden trunks, sacks, and baskets in a number of secret locations, one of which is believed to be in a cave near Kingston, New Hampshire, in Rockingham County. In fact, in 1903 a diligent search for this cave was conducted, but turned up little more than a few incidental Indian artifacts . . . and no cave.

Another region said to house more ill-gotten Indian loot is Stub Hill, near Pittsburg, in northern Coos County. Though the details of this location are also fuzzy, the story surrounding the stashed cash is corroborated by firsthand accounts. A handful of English prisoners had been marched to Canada by their Indian captors and were later ransomed. During the march, they saw two Indians struggling under the weight of a large iron cookpot, bouncing heavy and full on a wooden pole they had carried between them. In time, they detoured off the trail and disappeared into the woods at the base of Stub Hill. Soon the two Indians, noticeably happier without their cumbersome load, returned to the march and continued the journey to Canada.

* * *

Yet another White Mountain treasure tale that bears repeating—whether true or merely a teased-out tassel of tantalizing treasure-hunter's lore has yet to be proven—is that of the incredible lost necklace of Marie Antoinette. (Yes, that Marie Antoinette, queen of France from 1774 to 1792, and the very woman so frequently quoted as saying, "Let them eat cake"—though there is no proof she ever uttered the oft-said phrase. It is instead considered a journalistic fabrication.)

Linguistic history aside, how does the queen of France figure into the history of New Hampshire? So the (admittedly vague) story goes, in the days leading up to the French Revolution, the flamboyant queen instructed her country's leading jeweler to craft an exquisite diamond necklace—valued, as it turned out, at six million pounds. That's some choker!

It is said that the necklace ended up smuggled to Canada with exiled royals. Once there, it dropped from record books and other than an acknowledgment that a high-priced necklace belonging to the queen was among the missing, no official mention of it was ever again made.

But . . . a century later, an Indian and his Frenchman friend trekked south of the border and built a cabin alongside the road leading to Pennichuck Pond near Nashua, New Hampshire. Periodically the Indian returned to Canada to visit family, but his French companion was a homebody and rarely ventured beyond their homestead.

Following one of his visits north, the Indian returned to the cabin to find that his old friend had died. The Indian fell into a funk and mourned for days, then simply walked away. A number of years later, he returned as suddenly as he had vanished. And he was once again seen roving the banks of Pennichuck Pond.

Some of the locals remembered him and his French companion, and he inquired about a certain glittering object that the Frenchman had been secretly entrusted years before to watch over. The Indian referred to it only as a stunning thing of rare beauty and exceedingly high value. He said they had buried it along the shore of the pond many years before, and that he had been searching high and low for it, but could not recall with any accuracy the spot where they had buried it. He and others searched for many moons, but failed to turn up sign of the purportedly royal bauble.

Was it the fabled lost necklace commissioned by Marie Antoinette sent to Canada for safekeeping? Or was it some other bit of wealth that the two friends had spent long years watching over? While we may never know, one thing is for certain—whatever the two men buried so long ago along the shore of tranquil Pennichuck Pond, nothing of the sort has ever been reported found there. And French records from the Revolution show that a valuable necklace belonging to the queen was indeed lost in the struggle, and is still considered among the missing.

* * *

In Hillsborough, there is a twin-arch bridge, known as the Old Carr Bridge, that spans Beard's Brook. The idea for it was conceived by handsome militia captain Jonathan Carr, who also charitably paid for its construction in 1840. At first blush, this magnanimous gesture was most appreciated locally. But problems soon arose when he paid the carpenters and other laborers on the job with counterfeit cash, cash that he himself printed. It seems that Carr and a few of his cohorts ran a tidy little counterfeiting ring out of a cave not far from Carr's Hillsborough home.

When the falseness behind his largesse was discovered, he was arrested and a search of his home turned up great stacks of funny money. The same was found in that cave close by Carr's home. But the plates used to print the money were never found.

Well known locally, though not necessarily well regarded, the dashing, broad-shouldered Captain Carr nonetheless didn't rat out his fellow counterfeiters. At his trial he was told by the judge to lower his head in humility to receive his sentence. Carr is said to have replied: "God almighty made me to look man in the face."

"So be it," said the judge. And for that, Carr spent the first nineteen months of his ten-year sentence in solitary confinement—with his head chained down! Even after all that, the plates were never found. But the bridge he paid for with his funny money still stands today.

CHAPTER 12

The Saga of Ocean-Born Mary

A Baby, a Pirate, a House, and a Huckster

J ames Wilson stood and stretched his back. "I'm going to go up on deck for a bit of fresh air." He smiled at his tired wife and the sleeping three-day-old baby in her lap. Then his face grew serious again and he leaned close to his wife's rosy face and whispered, "I'll only be a moment. I want to talk with the captain, see what all this shouting is about."

As he turned to go, she gripped his arm. "James, you know what this crew has proven to be like—they shout about every-thing. Promise me you won't anger the captain. He's doing his best to get us there in a timely fashion."

"I know, my dear, but these are unsafe waters, and besides"—he winked back at her—"I'm a family man now. It's my duty to pay attention to such things."

The sounds of men bellowing at one another, much louder now, interrupted him and everyone looked upward. James

Wilson took the stairs two at a time. And what he saw froze him—a ship, and so close he could see men aboard her. Why had they not raised the alarm sooner?

"Pirates," he muttered, eyeing the approaching ship. She was a long, sleek frigate, and she bore a dark look as she coursed into full view. As Wilson counted the jostling and scurrying figures lining the deck of the fast-approaching ship, a belching ring of black smoke erupted from amidships, high up on her near side. Seconds later he heard the resounding *ka-thump!* of a cannon blast. He heard the sizzling rush of the projectile as a ball punched a tattered hole through their mainsail and dove into the briny deep fifty yards beyond their own ship, the *Wolf.*

Even as he thought to himself that they had just received a pirate's dire warning, a thin young deck hand beside him muttered, "Them's pirates, they are. Oh dear, oh dear. Me mum warned me about taking to the sea. She said I'd not last long enough to worry about." The youth's eye corners jounced and his lips trembled.

"But I reckon she were wrong, because I'm still here, ain't I? I mean, them pirates ain't killed us yet."

Not yet, thought James, pushing past the still-rambling youth, worry filling him as his own ship's captain bellowed orders and sent deck hands scurrying.

The pirate ship bristled with guns and leering men and looked to be capable of tearing them to pieces. There was no outrunning them. And then he heard a baby's cry rising up from belowdecks. "Elizabeth!" he said, pushing past the captain to get to his wife.

"I wish to God they could have waited 'til Boston. A crying bairn is all I need at a time like this!" The captain shook his head and continued stalking the deck of the ship he knew he'd soon lose to the foul pirates.

* * *

It didn't take long before the notorious Captain Pedro, a pirate whose reputation for harsh treatment of his captives, climbed aboard the *Wolf.* He was preceded by a host of his minions, hard-looking sailors with sneers slashing their mouths wide, revealing rotted teeth.

"Drag them all abovedecks and bind fast their hands and feet. I'll not have anyone lunging into the sea before I've had a chance to deal with them myself." The tall, lean Captain Pedro's hearty laughter was soon followed by peals of the same from his men. They busied themselves jerking to their knees all the captives they could easily grab.

As four men, daggers and cutlasses drawn, headed for the stairs that led belowdecks, the lusty cry of a baby echoed up the stairs. It raged but a moment more before it ceased abruptly, as if someone had clapped a quieting hand over the wee thing's mouth.

"What is that?" The pirate turned to the *Wolf*'s captain. "A new baby?"

The captain's rapid nods confirmed the pirate's question. In response, Pedro merely grunted at the trembling man and, drawing his cutlass, elbowed past his dumbfounded men. Belowdecks, and down a short hallway, he stopped before a closed cabin door, hearing the soft sounds of a woman's voice as if pleading in a whisper.

One corner of his mouth rose, his black moustache bristling with it, and quickly trying the door handle, found it locked. He raised a mighty black boot and kicked once, twice, something in the door snapped, wood cracked, and it spasmed inward. A young woman lay in a bunk within, clutching a baby to her bare breast, offering it succor, no doubt in an effort to quell the child's cries.

Suddenly a thin, pale man lunged at the pirate, who was too taken by surprise to do much more than raise an arm in defense.

"Leave my family be!"

By then Pedro had regained his composure and held his blade before him, its tip aimed at the sickly man's chest. "And if I do not?"

"I will kill you," said James Wilson.

The pirate snorted a laugh. "With what? You are unarmed, sir."

Wilson could only sneer at Pedro, hatred sparking his eyes in an otherwise pale face. His hands clenched in thin fists.

"Up on deck with you."

"No. I will not leave my wife and child to the likes of you."

Pedro smiled and pushed the cutlass blade against Wilson's chest. From the bunk, Elizabeth shouted, "No, do not hurt my husband, please! James, do as he says. Please."

"She is wise," said Pedro. "And you would be, too, if you followed her advice." He sighed and his smile slipped. "I will not harm them."

"I do not trust you," said James.

"And I have given you no reason to think you should."

Just then, two hard-looking characters poked their faces in beside Pedro. "You'll be wanting our help, Cap'n?"

"Yes, take this man on deck. But"—he turned to the woman in the bunk—"see that no harm comes to him."

As the three struggling men left them, Elizabeth's eyes were drawn impossibly wide, but she held tight to her baby and did her best to keep from screaming at the sight of the foul pirate.

The pirate, with cutlass poised as if ready to strike, stared down at her, not quite smiling. "Madam, I find you have placed me in a curious situation." The pirate's gaze pinned her to the spot as she stroked her new baby's head.

"I . . . I did not mean to do so, sir," said Elizabeth, not knowing what else to say.

Suddenly Captain Pedro smiled again, and the effect it had on his countenance was remarkable. He shifted his gaze to the now much quieted little pink face, and he smiled at it, despite his efforts to remain aloof.

"Is it christened?"

"No, no, sir, she is barely three days old."

"Born aboardships, eh?" He lowered his blade.

She merely nodded, trying to keep from trembling as she covered her baby's head with her hand, stroking softly.

"Good mother, grant me one favor and I will desist from my original intention of the harm I had intended toward everyone onboard this ship, and to the ship itself."

"I . . . I don't understand."

"Madam, I wish you would consider granting me a request. In return, I will spare the lives of all aboard this bucket."

Elizabeth Wilson, not quite knowing what he meant, could only nod dumbly, convinced that at any moment his trickery would reveal itself. Oh, what of James? What had they done to him? "Anything," she said, biting back her fear, doubting that his word was worth a thing, but feeling no choice in the matter.

"Promise me you will name this baby girl after my own sainted mother, God rest her soul."

Elizabeth was about to ask what the pirate's mother's name might be, when he offered the very name himself, as if he had read her mind.

"Mary, she was, and though she is no longer with us, I ask that you name your child after my mother."

Elizabeth stared at him, not quite comprehending what was happening.

"Excellent. I name the child Ocean-Born Mary." Captain Pedro straightened and sniffed once. "And so it is said and done."

Pedro fixed the trembling young mother with his steely gaze, as if awaiting her agreement.

She nodded solemnly.

He drew in breath as if he were about to launch into a windy speech, but said nothing. Then the pirate leaned forward and, with a long, begrimed finger, he lightly touched the now-silent baby girl's forehead, then her wee hand.

He backed away a step, lifted off his feathered tri-corn, and offered her an elaborate bow. "I have something for the child." He turned and departed the room, but hadn't gone a step when he leaned back in and said, "Don't go anywhere." His short bark of laughter only served to tighten the knot in her throat.

Elizabeth heard voices above, tried to make out her husband's but could not. She discerned but a few stray words— "kill us" and "Oh God," were among the more popular. Pedro returned shortly with a thick bolt of fine quality Chinese silk, its elaborate embroidery standing out against the light green of the cloth.

"This, my dear mother, is for Ocean-Born Mary's wedding day. Nothing but the best for her gown, you see." He laid the sizable bolt of cloth beside Elizabeth. Once more, he touched the back of the now-sleeping baby's little pink hand and with a slight smile, departed.

She heard his steps recede, heard his boots clump resoundingly off the planking above. She heard a volley of angry shouts, presumably from his men, that hushed abruptly with a growl of anger from him. Soon enough, Elizabeth heard the creaking, rattling sounds of the pirate ship departing, its great sails luffing, and then snapping tight with a bellyful of wind. Soon her husband made his way back down belowdecks and their mutual relief was palpable in their dim quarters.

The young mother and her tiny baby were celebrated by the passengers and lauded by the captain for saving their lives. And

The "Ocean Born Mary" House, Henniker, N. H. Built 1780.

Postal card, Ocean-Born Mary House; Gravestone photograph by Jennifer Smith-Mayo

Top: Though this home is known as Ocean-Born Mary House, there is no evidence its namesake ever visited there, let alone lived there. But that didn't prevent a later owner from spinning tall tales about pirates, buried treasure in the orchard, and the ghost of Mary herself. Below: Despite the falsehoods, there was indeed a woman named Ocean-Born Mary, and her gravestone can be found in Henniker's Centre Cemetery, just behind the Henniker Town Hall.

true to her word, despite the captain's insistence that the promise to a pirate was no thing meant for keeping, Elizabeth boldly stated that on reaching Boston, her baby would be christened Ocean-Born Mary. The child, after all, had saved their lives. In exchange, Elizabeth and James agreed the least they could do was to honor their end of the bargain.

But Mary's mother's troubles were not over. Shortly after docking in Boston, Elizabeth's husband, James Wilson, succumbed to the creeping sickness that had rendered him nearly incapacitated during the long, tedious journey from Londonderry, Ireland. Fortunately for young Mary and her mother, a number of their fellow passengers were headed up the coast to Londonderry, New Hampshire, to settle with friends and family. She assumed the land that had been granted to her husband, as he had been a grantee of the town. There, Elizabeth and Ocean-Born Mary found a warm and welcoming community of friends only too glad to help care for the child who had saved so many. (Incidentally, Elizabeth later married James Clark, great-great-grandfather of famous newspaperman and politician Horace Greeley, himself an Amherst, New Hampshire, native and one of two men to have allegedly uttered the phrase, "Go West, young man, go West and grow up with the country.")

The strange saga of this unwitting savior of a ship full of poor immigrants could have ended there and still made the history books. But it did not, for Mary's life sailed on, and offered yet more interesting and unusual dips and directions. She grew to become a beautiful young Scots-Irish woman, six feet tall, and was said to have lustrous, long red hair, sparkling green eyes, and a sprinkling of freckles on her unblemished skin.

And on December 18, 1742, she put to use the offering Captain Pedro had given her mother for one express purpose. Mary wedded James Wallace (some accounts refer to him as Thomas, though his gravestone marks him as James), wearing a fine gown made of Captain Pedro's gifted light green brocaded silk.

She and James went on to have four sons and a daughter. Three of the sons married three sisters and settled in Henniker. Her daughter, Elizabeth, married Lieutenant Thomas Patterson of the New Hampshire Militia. (Elizabeth knitted her betrothed white stockings for their wedding, beginning a tradition in which those stockings were worn by male Pattersons on their wedding day up until 1966, when they were last worn, then donated to the New Hampshire Historical Society, no doubt in need of a good darning.)

Mary and James lived a long life together in Londonderry. On October 30, 1791, her husband died at the age of eighty-one. (He is buried at the Old Hill Graveyard in Londonderry, and though his marker mentions Mary, she is not buried with him.) On his death, Mary was seventy-one. In 1798, when she was seventy-eight, she moved to Henniker to live with her son, William, and his family, with whom she resided for the final sixteen years of her life. She was a busy woman until her death on February 13, 1814, at age ninety-four. She is buried in the family plot of her son, William, at the Centre Cemetery in Henniker, located behind the Henniker Town Hall. In fact, her grave can be found on the right side of the cemetery, twelve rows in from the front gate.

That's where much of the known truth of Ocean-Born Mary's tale ends. What follows is legend, shaded by hucksterism, superstition, and lots of fine old New England tall-tale telling.

* * *

Many years earlier, so the hard-to-believe but equally hard-to-resist story goes, the old pirate who had given Mary her name (he is, depending on the account one chooses to pursue, either notorious pirate Philip Babb, or Captain Pedro, aka Don Pedro) had finagled a pardon from the government for his piratical activities, presumably through political payoffs and bribery. The old buccaneer commissioned a finely appointed home built for him in the small town of Henniker, as a retreat now that his pillaging days were behind him.

He is said to have persuaded Mary and her young sons and daughter to keep house for him in exchange for a fine roof over their heads. He also apparently had amorous intentions that may have been reciprocated by Mary. Hmm. This spur of the Ocean-Born Mary legend fails to take into account the fact that Mary's husband lived to the age of eighty-one, all the while happily married to Mary, long after their children had grown and raised families of their own.

Furthermore, this version states that in the pirate's later years—which would place him roughly at the century mark—an aged Mary was presumably happy as a clam tending to him in his Henniker hideaway. One evening, the pirate was lured outside to his orchard, suspecting someone was snooping where they ought not, and about to discover the spot where he had buried his pirate loot. From inside, Mary heard a terrible commotion, and by the time she made it outside to see what had happened, she found the old pirate dead in the orchard, stabbed through with a cutlass, no less. Poetic touch, that

It has also been said that Mary continued to live in the pirate's house, the very house that today is known as the Ocean-Born Mary House. Well, there is a house called the Ocean-Born Mary House. But she never lived there. Not with a geriatric pirate or alone. Her son Richard, from whom she was estranged, lived there. There is no proof that Mary ever even visited that house.

Much of what has come to be considered Ocean-Born Mary lore was fabricated by a man named Louis Maurice Auguste Roy. In 1917 Roy bought the old Wallace House, once owned by Mary's son Robert. By the early twentieth century, it had become a dilapidated, unoccupied place. Mr. Roy moved there from Wisconsin with his mother and spent much time and money fixing up the place. In the process, Mr. Roy learned of the story of Ocean-Born Mary and decided that his abode's tenuous connection entitled him to exploit the legend six ways from Sunday, conjuring whatever elements served to suit his purposes.

He opened his house to the public, for a nominal fee, naturally, and proceeded to spin a stack of tall tales about the wondrous life of Mary and her pirate benefactor. He told of the ghosts of both Mary and the pirate roaming the house and grounds, and of the buried pirate loot, still unfound somewhere about the orchard. Of unknown bodies buried beneath a massive, mysterious rock slab forming the fireplace hearth. . . .

And what of the pirate? Despite all the stories, there is no record of any such person ever buying land in Henniker, let alone burying loot in an orchard and then dying of a saber wound. Their age disparity would have made the old sea dog a century or more old. But the indefatigable Mr. Roy had lit up a powerful thing— the public's imagination, and its urge to believe the fantastic over the mundane.

The more bizarre and ghostly Roy made the stories, the better the public liked them, even when they knew he was full of beans. Most of his tales were woven out of whole cloth, with the help of such shameless, albeit fun and effective, devices as Mary's rocking chair that rocked of its own accord. Never mind that the wily Roy rocked the chair with the help of a loose floorboard.

Roy even rented out shovels for fifty cents to eager treasure hunters who thought they might strike it rich in his old orchard. Surely logic would have told potential diggers that Roy would already have dug up his property if he truly believed he had pirate treasure buried in his back yard. . . .

Mr. Roy's success in conveying his fabrications was so complete that even the Russells, a couple who came, in his dotage, to care for him and subsequently to live in the house themselves, were hounded for years by people who refused to believe that Roy had made up all those tales of ghosts and buried pirate treasure.

For decades, strangers trespassed day and night, broke into the house, stole items, and caused all manner of havoc in what is still known as Ocean-Born Mary House—which is not haunted by the ghost of the woman who never lived there.

That's not to say she never existed. As we know, there was indeed a woman known as Ocean-Born Mary, she did wear a beautiful green dress on her wedding day, allegedly made of silk given to her mother for that express purpose by a pirate who had abstained that long-ago day of July 28, 1720, from killing the ship full of passengers not far from Boston Harbor. The dress was worn subsequently by a number of Mary's descendants, and scraps from it reside in the D.A.R. Museum in Washington, DC, and at the Henniker Public Library.

Much of the fascination of this story comes from the variety of versions that share basic facts but differ in a number of telling details, not unlike most episodes lost to history. So, is the strange, compelling, spooky, mystical, intriguing, adventure- and love-filled tale of the life and times of Ocean-Born Mary true, real, and legitimate? That all depends on who you ask and what you choose to believe—and how many ways you believe a story can be told. In the case of Ocean-Born Mary, the jury's still out. Or is it?

No matter how much or how little of the story you believe, a visit to the grave of Ocean-Born Mary the next time you're in Henniker is a fine way to spend time with a legitimate legend. The house that she never lived in (and therefore doesn't haunt), however, is a private residence and is decidedly not open to the public.

BIBLIOGRAPHY

Abbott, Geoffrey. *The Executioner Always Chops Twice: Ghastly Blunders on the Scaffold.* New York: St. Martin's Press, 2002.

Baker, Emerson W. *The Devil of Great Island: Witchcraft and Conflict in Early New England.* New York: Palgrave Macmillan, 2007.

Balkan, Evan. *Shipwrecked! Deadly Adventures and Disasters at Sea.* Birmingham, AL: Menasha Ridge, 2008.

Beckius, Kim Knox. *Backroads of New England: Your Guide to New England's Most Scenic Backroad Adventures.* St. Paul, MN: Voyageur Press/MBI Publishing, 2004.

Belanger, Jeff, ed. *Encyclopedia of Haunted Places: Ghostly Locales from Around the World.* Edison, NJ: Castle Books, 2008.

Bell, Michael E. *Food for the Dead: On the Trail of New England's Vampires.* New York: Carroll & Graf Publishers, 2001.

Bellamy, John Stark, III. *Vintage Vermont Villainies: True Tales of Murder and Mystery from 19th and 20th Centuries.* Woodstock, VT: Countryman Press, 2007.

Bellesiles, Michael A. *Revolutionary Outlaws: Ethan Allen and the Struggle for Independence on the Early American Frontier.* Charlottesville: University Press of Virginia, 1993.

Binder, Jeff. *New Hampshire* (Compass American Guides). New York: Fodor's, 2002.

Blanton, DeAnne, and Lauren M. Cook. *They Fought Like Demons: Women Soldiers in the American Civil War.* Baton Rouge: Louisiana State University Press, 2002.

Bondeson, Jan. *The Great Pretenders: The True Stories Behind Famous Historical Mysteries.* New York: W.W. Norton & Co., 2004.

Bryson, Bill. *The Lost Continent: Travels in Small-Town America.* New York: Harper Perennial, 1990.

Burr, George Lincoln, ed. *Narratives of the Witchcraft Cases, 1648–1706, Volume 16.* New York: Charles Scribner's Sons, 1914.

Campbell, Susan, and Bruce Gellerman. *The Big Book of New England Curiosities: From Orange, CT, to Blue Hill, ME, a Guide to the Quirkiest, Oddest, and Most Unbelievable Stuff You'll See.* Guilford, CT: Globe Pequot Press, 2009.

Chenoweth, James. *Oddity Odyssey: A Journey Through New England's Colorful Past.* New York: Henry Holt, 1996.

Citro, Joseph A. *Passing Strange: True Tales of New England Hauntings and Horrors*. Shelburne, VT: Chapters Publishing, 1996.

———. *Weird New England*. New York: Sterling Publishing Co., 2005.

Clifford, Barry. *Expedition* Whydah: *The Story of the World's First Excavation of a Pirate Treasure Ship and the Man Who Found Her*. New York: HarperCollins Publishers, 1999.

Coleman, Loren and Huyghe, Patrick. *The Field Guide to Bigfoot, Yeti, and Other Mystery Primates Worldwide*. New York: Avon Books, 1999.

Cordingly, David. *Women Sailors and Sailors' Women*. New York: Random House, 2001.

Cronon, William. *Changes in the Land: Indians, Colonists and the Ecology of New England*. New York: Hill and Wang/Farrar-Straus & Giroux, 1983.

Dickerman, Mike, and Steve D. Smith. *Mount Washington: A Short Guide and History*. Littleton, NH: Bondcliff Books, 2007.

Druett, John. *She Captains: Heroines and Hellions of the Sea*. New York: Simon & Schuster, 2000.

Feintuch, Burt, and David H. Watters, eds. *The Encyclopedia of New England*. New Haven, CT: Yale University Press, 2005.

Felton, Bruce, and Mark Fowler. *Felton & Fowler's Famous Americans You Never Knew Existed*. New York: Stein and Day, 1979.

Fleming, Thomas. *Liberty! The American Revolution*. New York: Viking/Penguin, 1997.

Fowler, William W. *Frontier Women*. Stamford, CT: Longmeadow Press, 1995.

Freedman, Lew. *The Way We Were New England: Nostalgic Images of America's Northeast*. Guilford, CT: Globe Pequot Press, 2009.

Friedman, Stanton T., and Kathleen Marden. *Captured! The Betty and Barney Hill UFO Experience*. Franklin Lakes, NJ: New Page Books, 2007.

Fuller, John G. *Incident at Exeter*. New York: G. P. Putnam's Sons, 1974.

———. *The Interrupted Journey*. New York: Dell, 1987.

Ginsburg, Philip E. *The Shadow of Death: The Hunt for a Serial Killer*. New York: Charles Scribner's Sons, 1991.

Goldberg, M. Hirsh. *The Blunder Book*. New York: William Morrow & Co., 1984.

Green, Stewart M. *Scenic Routes & Byways: New England*. Guilford, CT: Globe Pequot Press, 2012.

Hall, David D. *Witch-Hunting in Seventeenth-Century New England: A Documentary History 1638–1693*. Durham, NC: Duke University Press, 1999.

Hall, Richard. *Patriots in Disguise: Women Warriors of the Civil War*. New York: Paragon House, 1993.

Hansen, Harry, ed. *New England Legends and Folklore*. New York: Hastings House, 1967.

Hauck, Dennis William. *Haunted Places: The National Directory.* New York: Penguin Group, 2002.

Hawthorne, Nathaniel. *The Story of the Great Stone Face.* Littleton, NH: Sherwin/Dodge Printers.

Higginson, Thomas Wentworth. *Travelers and Outlaws: Episodes in American History.* New York: Lee and Shepard, 1889.

Hill, Ralph Nading. *Yankee Kingdom: Vermont and New Hampshire.* New York: Harper & Bros., 1960.

Holland, Barbara. *Brief Histories & Heroes.* Pleasantville, NY: Akadine Press, 1998.

Johnson, Claudia Durst. *Daily Life in Colonial New England.* Westport, CT: Greenwood Press, 2002.

Johnson, Dorothy M., and R. T. Turner. *The Bedside Book of Bastards: A Rich Collection of Counterirritants to the Exasperations of Contemporary Life.* New York: Barnes & Noble Books, 1994.

Jones, Eric. *New Hampshire Curiosities: Quirky Characters, Roadside Oddities & Other Offbeat Stuff.* Guilford, CT: Globe Pequot Press, 2006.

Jordan, Charles J. *Tales Told in the Shadows of the White Mountains.* Lebanon, NH: University Press of New England, 2003.

Mack, John E., MD. *Passport to the Cosmos: Human Transformation and Alien Encounters.* Three Rivers Press, 1999.

Mayo, Matthew P. *Bootleggers, Lobstermen, and Lumberjacks: Fifty of the Grittiest Moments in the History of Hardscrabble New England.* Guilford, CT: Globe Pequot Press, 2011.

McCain, Diana Ross. *Mysteries and Legends of New England: True Stories of the Unsolved and Unexplained.* Guilford, CT: Globe Pequot Press, 2009.

McDevitt, Neale, ed. *Eyewitness Travel Guides New England.* New York: Dorling Kindersley Publishing, Inc., 2001.

Morgan, Edmund S. *American Heroes: Profiles of Men and Women Who Shaped Early America.* New York: W.W. Norton & Co., 2009.

Morison, Samuel Eliot. *The Maritime History of Massachusetts 1783–1860.* Boston, MA: Northeastern University Press, 1979.

Murray, Stuart. *Eyewitness Books: American Revolution.* New York: Dorling Kindersley Publishing, 2002.

New England: A Collection from Harper's Magazine. New York: Gallery Books, 1990.

New England (DK Eyewitness Travel). London, UK: DK Books, 2007.

Ocker, J. W. *The New England Grimpendium: A Guide to Macabre and Ghastly Sites.* Woodstock, VT: Countryman Press, 2010.

O'Connor, Marianne. *Haunted Hikes of New Hampshire.* Exeter, NH: PublishingWorks, 2008.

Oppel, Frank., ed. *Tales of the New England Coast.* Secaucus, NJ: Castle Books, 1985.

Pettengill, Samuel B. *The Yankee Pioneers: A Saga of Courage.* Rutland, VT: Charles E. Tuttle Co., 1971.

Philips, David E. *Legendary Connecticut: Traditional Tales from the Nutmeg State.* Willimantic, CT: Curbstone Press, 1992.

Pike, Robert, E. *Spiked Boots.* Dublin, NH: Yankee Books, 1987.

———. *Tall Trees, Tough Men.* New York: W. W. Norton, 1999.

Platt, Camille Smith. *Real Cheesy Facts About: Famous Authors.* Birmingham, AL: Crane Hill Publishers, 2006.

Quinn, William P. *Shipwrecks Around New England: A Chronology of Marine Accidents and Disasters from Grand Manan to Sandy Hook.* Orleans, MA: Lower Cape Publishing, 1979.

Ramsey, Floyd W. *The Willey Slide: A New Chronicle of the Famous Tragedy in Ample Detail and Soberly Recounted.* Littleton, NH: Bondcliff Books, 2009.

Rapaport, Diane. *The Naked Quaker: True Crimes and Controversies from the Courts of Colonial New England.* Beverly, MA: Commonwealth Editions, 2007.

Rogak, Lisa. *Stones and Bones of New England: A Guide to Unusual, Historic, and Otherwise Notable Cemeteries.* Guilford, CT: Globe Pequot Press, 2004.

Rogers, Barbara Radcliffe, and Stillman Rogers. *New Hampshire Off the Beaten Path.* Guilford, CT: Globe Pequot Press, 2002.

Rogers, Stillman. *It Happened in New Hampshire: Remarkable Events that Shaped History.* Guilford, CT: Globe Pequot Press, 2012.

Rondina, Christopher. *Vampires of New England.* Cape Cod, MA: On Cape Publications, 2008.

Russell, Howard S. *A Long, Deep Furrow: Three Centuries of Farming in New England.* Hanover, NH: University Press of New England, 1982.

Schlosser, S. E. *Spooky New England: Tales of Hauntings, Strange Happenings, and Other Local Lore.* Guilford, CT: Globe Pequot Press, 2003.

Sherr, Lynn, and Jurate Kazickas. *Susan B. Anthony Slept Here: A Guide to American Women's Landmarks.* New York: Times Books/Random House, 1994.

Simons, D. Brenton. *Witches, Rakes, and Rogues: True Stories of Scam, Scandal, Murder, and Mayhem in Boston, 1630–1775.* Beverly, MA: Commonwealth Editions, 2005.

Sloane, Eric. *Diary of an Early American Boy: Noah Blake, 1805.* New York: Ballantine Books, 1965.

Smith, Joshua M. *Borderland Smuggling: Patriots, Loyalists, and Illicit Trade in the Northeast, 1783–1820.* Gainesville: University Press of Florida, 2006.

Smithsonian Guide to Historic America: Southern New England. New York: Stewart, Tabori & Chang, 1989.

Snow, Edward Rowe. *Ghosts, Gales and Gold.* New York: Dodd, Mead & Co., 1972.

———. *Tales of Terror and Tragedy.* New York: Dodd, Mead, and Co., 1980.

Stanley, Jo, ed. *Bold in Her Breeches: Women Pirates Across the Ages.* New York: HarperCollins, 1995.

Stanway, Eric. *The Old Rindge House: An Examination of a New Hampshire Legend.* Fitzwilliam, NH: Author, 2012.

St. Antoine, Sara, ed. *Stories from Where We Live: The North Atlantic Coast.* Minneapolis, MN: Milkweed Editions, 2000.

Starbuck, David R., ed. *Historical New Hampshire* 49, no. 4 (Winter 1994). Concord: New Hampshire Historical Society, 1994.

Stephens, John Richard, ed. *Captured by Pirates: 22 Firsthand Accounts of Murder and Mayhem on the High Seas.* New York: Barnes & Noble, 2006.

Stevens, Peter F. *Notorious & Notable New Englanders.* Camden, ME: Down East Books, 1997.

Taylor, Troy. *Out Past the Campfire Light.* Alton, IL: Whitechapel Productions Press, 2004.

Thornton, Brian. *The Book of Bastards: 101 Worst Scoundrels and Scandals from the World of Politics and Power.* Avon, MA: Adams Media, 2010.

Titler, Dale M. *Unnatural Resources: True Stories of American Treasure.* Englewood Cliffs, NJ: Prentice-Hall, 1973.

Vaughan, Alden T. *New England Encounters: Indians and Euroamericans, ca. 1600–1850.* Lebanon, NH: University Press of New England, 1999.

———. *New England Frontier: Puritans and Indians 1620–1675.* Norman: University of Oklahoma Press, 1995.

Weir, William. *Written With Lead: America's Most Famous and Notorious Gunfights from the Revolutionary War to Today.* New York: Cooper Square Press, 2003.

Wheeler, Scott. *Rumrunners & Revenuers.* Shelburne, VT: New England Press, 2002.

Wiencek, Henry. *The Smithsonian Guide to Historic America: Southern New England.* New York: Stewart, Tabori & Chang, 1989.

Wilbur, C. Keith, MD. *New England Indians, 2nd ed.: An Informed and Fascinating Account of the 18 Major Tribes that Lived in Pre-Colonial New England.* Guilford, CT: Globe Pequot Press, 1996.

Woodard, Colin. *The Republic of Pirates: Being the True and Surprising Story of the Caribbean Pirates and the Man Who Brought Them Down.* New York: Harcourt, 2007.

Zinn, Howard. *A People's History of the United States.* New York: HarperCollins Publishers, 2003.

INDEX

ABOUT THE AUTHOR

Matthew P. Mayo is an award-winning author, and has written more than twenty-five books and dozens of short stories. His novel, *Tucker's Reckoning*, won the Western Writers of America's 2013 Spur Award for Best Western Novel. He has also been a Spur finalist in the Short Fiction category and a Western Fictioneers Peacemaker Award finalist. His novels include *Winters' War*; *Wrong Town*; *Hot Lead, Cold Heart*; *Dead Man's Ranch*; *The Hunted*; and many more. He also contributes to other popular series of Western and adventure novels.

Matthew's nonfiction books include *Cowboys, Mountain Men & Grizzly Bears*; *Bootleggers, Lobstermen & Lumberjacks*; *Sourdoughs, Claim Jumpers & Dry Gulchers*; *Haunted Old West*; *Speaking Ill of the Dead: Jerks in New England History* (all TwoDot/Globe Pequot Press); and numerous others. He has collaborated with his wife, photographer Jennifer Smith-Mayo, on a series of hardcover books by Globe Pequot Press, including *Maine Icons*, *New Hampshire Icons*, and *Vermont Icons*.

The Mayos also run Gritty Press (GrittyPress.com) and rove North America in their pickup truck and Airstream trailer in search of hot coffee, tasty whiskey, and high adventure. Stop by Matthew's website for a chin-wag and a cup of joe at MatthewMayo.com.

CPSIA information can be obtained
at www.ICGtesting.com
Printed in the USA
LVHW082206260619
622495LV00033B/528/P